PROGRAM EVALUATION
GUIDELINES

PROGRAM EVALUATION
GUIDELINES

A Research Handbook
for Agency Personnel

Joyce L. Sichel, Ph.D.

HUMAN SCIENCES PRESS,INC.
72 FIFTH AVENUE,
NEW YORK, N.Y. 10011

066451

Printed in the United States of America
23456789   987654321

Library of Congress Cataloging in Publication Data

Sichel, Joyce L.
  Program evaluation guidelines.

  Bibliography
  Includes index.
1. Evaluation research (social action programs)
I. Title.
H61.S555   361.6'1'072   LC 81–4148
ISBN 0-89885-030-4   AACR2

CONTENTS

Preface   7
1. WHY YOUR AGENCY MIGHT WANT TO BOTHER
   WITH EVALUATION   9
      To Answer Real Questions About Programs   9
      To Satisfy Powers-That-Be   11
      To Carry Out Hidden Agendas   12
2. "BUT WE ALREADY KEEP STATISTICS!"   15
      Information Systems vs. Informative Answers   15
      Is Your Data Good Enough?   18
      Potential for Evaluations Using Information
         Systems   20
3. REINVENTING THE WHEEL—HOW TO AVOID IT   25
      Check Out Prior Studies in the "Annals" of Your
         Agency   25
      Find Out What Other Agencies Have Done   27
      Join Up With Complementary Groups   28
      Take Advantage of Publications, Reports, and
         Computer Programs   29
      Get Experience on Your Team   30

4. BALLPARK EVALUATION PLANNING YOU CAN DO   32
        Let the Nature of Your Questions Define a Focus   32
        Let the Nature of Your Questions Dictate the Scope
            of Your Research   33
        Matters of Timing   34
        Guessing About Methods   35
        Some Representative "Ballparks"   36
5. SHOULD YOU CALL IN THE EXPERTS?   38
        Getting Help With Your Evaluation Thinking   38
        Having the Experts Collect Your Data   39
        Help With the Numbers   39
        Do You Need a Writer?   40
        Eenie, Meenie . . .   40
        Outsiders Should Become Honorary Insiders   42
        Contracting for the Work   43
        The In-House Alternative   44
6. WHAT SHOULD IT COST AND WHO WILL PAY?   48
        The Major Costs   48
        Getting Good People for Less Money   50
        Data Processing   52
        Money, Money   53
7. TALKING EVALUATIONESE   56
        Evaluationese Isn't Jargonese   56
        What a Few Key Terms Mean   57
        Why All the Fuss About Experiments?   60
8. DESIGNING EVALUATION SO THAT YOU GET SOME-
    THING USEFUL OUT OF IT   62
        Let Your Evaluation Questions Guide You   62
        Take Out Insurance on Usefulness   64
        Force Yourself to Look Ahead   65
9. LIKE, FOR INSTANCE . . .   67
        Before-and-After Studies   67
        Comparison-Group Studies   68
        Experiments   68
        Detailed Case Studies   69

Analysis of Program Costs 69
Other Approaches 70
10. LIVING THROUGH AN EVALUATION 72
Getting to the Nitty-Gritty 72
Lost in the Fields 73
Maintaining Control 73
Changes 74
Troubleshooting 75
11. "WHAT ARE ALL THOSE GREEK SYMBOLS?" 78
Computer Analyses 80
Do You Really Need a Computer? 81
What Does It All Mean? 81
12. THE END—IT DOESN'T HAVE TO BE BITTER 83
Previews of the Final Report 83
The Final Document 84
Spreading It Around 85
Notes 87
If You Want To Do Further Reading 89
Index 101

PREFACE

This handbook began as a way of helping out my friends in public agencies who became involved in evaluating the programs they designed and ran. I hoped to avert some panicked calls from nonresearchers who suddenly had to cope with a forbidding world of research requirements and "experts."

I offer the finished volume to my friends, but also to all of you who are program planners, department managers, or agency administrators who need the same kind of helping hand (even if it comes on published pages).

You need no research background to use this book. Good evaluation research, as I will continually stress, rests mainly on good common sense. I've written a small, informal book that you can read through in one long sitting and then refer back to as needed. I hope you will feel free to make notes in the margins.

One book won't make you an instant evaluation expert, but I hope it will enable you to take part in the evaluation planning process and to become a more confident evaluation participant. As a look at the chapter titles will suggest, I'll be stressing practical issues—how to frame guiding questions, how to define the appropriate scope for an evaluation, how to make sure you'll have something of use when you're done.

This book grew out of my personal experiences as a research social psychologist who has worked primarily with agencies in the criminal-justice field. I'll be telling you about many evaluation successes and failures I have experienced; I'll be giving examples from other fields that I think are interesting; and I'll be pointing out some of the pitfalls you should avoid. I hope you will find something in my experience and advice that will be useful to you and helpful in meeting your organization's evaluation needs in a responsible way.

Chapter 1

WHY YOUR AGENCY MIGHT WANT
TO BOTHER WITH EVALUATION

To Answer Real Questions About Programs

Coming up with informative, dependable answers to questions about programs that your organization runs is the best reason for bothering with evaluation research. Let's assume that you are an enlightened administrator who has taken an experimenting rather than advocacy posture with regard to specific new programs. You really care about whether they make sense. Questions begin in broad terms in your mind, like "How are we doing with our new (or old) program?" You can go on to framing the questions in a more specific and researchable manner: "Are our clients showing greater improvement (for example, in physical health, in mental health, in reading scores) with our new program than with traditional approaches?" "Do our procedures allow us to process more cases at lower cost than other agencies do?" "Has morale among our personnel improved since we instituted our organizational changes?" "Which of several approaches we have tried over the years has shown the longest-term benefits to our students (e.g.,

9

in gaining and keeping employment)?" These questions could all be starting points for evaluating the impact of your organization's programs.

You can also frame questions to evaluate the system tinkering you do while you're in the process of doing it. Here the pressing questions relate to program formulation rather than to ultimate program effects. Questions that initiate "formative," or operations-type, evaluation research might be: "Are there modifications we could make in our procedures that would lead to less dropping out from our new program?" or "Are our program services reaching those we want them to reach?" The pragmatism of these questions does not make them unworthy jumping-off places for research. Rather, questions of this nature can be excellent starting points for evaluations that will have immediate policy relevance.

Most of your program questions are likely to be value-related and to require value-related answers about program "goodness" or benefits or cost effectiveness. This is appropriate. I have personal knowledge of a federally funded "evaluation" system that for a long period of time was not really evaluative. It was set up to define common goals for sets of criminal-justice programs in New York State and to collect the same information on all programs in a set in order to measure each one's progress toward the defined goals. But when the system was first put into operation, while it described service programs adequately, it was unable to make evaluative statements about them. The decision makers who were to benefit from the system found that they knew all about the clients who had been served by the programs and the general types of services that had been provided. But they did *not* have research input on whether a program appeared to meet some minimum standards, whether it did its job or achieved results better than other programs or approaches, and whether it cost more or less than other programs to achieve what it did (New York State, Note 1). Good evaluation can describe programs, it can analyze procedures, it can study the processes that underly programs. But most importantly, it can evaluate.

What if you have no real questions about program effectiveness or operation? You may believe that a new study would only repeat old studies ad infinitum, and that, in any case, it would only tell you what you already know anyway. You may believe that talking to a few reliable operating personnel can answer all the questions you may have. Well, you could be right. Sometimes there are no real or new questions to address with evaluation. And sometimes talking to a few well-chosen staff members may tell you all you need to know about the programs your agency operates. Sometimes the value of a program has been demonstrated to everyone's satisfaction. Indeed, there probably have been more unneeded evaluation studies done than needed ones! But you don't want to miss those places where the questions dictate research. If you need to have highly reliable information to aid major decisions (such as choosing a program for widespread application), if you suspect that deeper probing might yield surprises (such as unintended side effects of a program), or if you need extensive information (such as quantitative changes over time or level of morale throughout your organization), you have real questions that evaluation research could help answer.

To Satisfy Powers-That-Be

In the real world, substantive questions may be secondary to the pushes and pulls of organizational hierarchies, interagency relationships, and governmental bureaucracy in getting evaluations started. There may be strong political pressure for program evaluation—the media may be demanding accountability from your organization or a fiscal crisis may have inspired a witch hunt for cost-ineffectiveness. You may suspect or know that unfavorable findings from a major impact evaluation could put your department or group out of business. Evaluations can conclude that programs are either unnecessary or uneconomical, or working poorly for some other reason. (But you may be relieved to know that few evaluations have results that are extreme enough to suggest program terminations.) How you handle pressures to conduct "life or death" evaluations will come from your normal management skills, rather than from any special research ones.

Pushes to evaluate can come from outside your organization too. Public agencies offering program funding may require that their programs be evaluated. They may provide you with both program funding and an evaluation "package"—budget lines for research, a consulting/technical assistance research group, and equipment. But they may also lock you contractually to research you consider irrelevant, burdensome, or unending; you may want to consider refusing funding when the strings attached to it are too great! At least try to get the funding source to allow your practical evaluation questions to have a prominent role in whatever research is to be undertaken. I had experience with a federal agency that was funding a new service for the elderly (D.H.E.W., Note 2). The funders asked for an elaborate experiment to evaluate the service. During the period of the experiment, clients' eligibility for the service was to be determined by whether they lived in odd- or even-numbered apartment buildings on New York City's Lower East Side. Because of the confusion and resentment this would have created among the elderly population to be served, the program operators rejected that kind of evaluation. Fortunately, it was possible to negotiate with the funding agency concerning the type of evaluation that would be done, and a different research design was developed that stressed operating issues and questions of particular concern to program staff.

To Carry Out Hidden Agendas

Some motives of powers-that-be are open and admitted; some are not, as with personal aggrandizement concerns and other organizational infighting. The boss may want publicity, or his nephew may need a job; there may be an existing research department to keep busy; heads of all the departments may be competing for new staff; your board of directors may urge program evaluation because they think it makes them look enlightened. See if you can interest some of these people in computers, rather than engaging in unnecessary program evaluations.

Our preconceptions and biases are even more subtle motives for getting into evaluation. Someone—and it could be you—might want to see a point of view "scientifically" demonstrated. Perhaps you believe that research will confirm for the world what your experience has taught you; or your president is confident that the programs run under his or her management will show up better than other approaches. These preconceptions are very common, so let's look at how they can affect the evaluation.

First, they may compromise the integrity of the evaluation work, or at least its objectivity. There have been numerous studies by psychologists and others of the ways that our biases can affect the outcome of research we do. You need not set out to bias the results for this to happen. (Rosenthal, Note 3). Your decisions about what data to collect, what measures to include and which to reject, and the way you interpret them can easily bend your findings to fit your point of view. It can happen merely by selecting a staff of people who are biased along your own lines (e.g., you, the school integration advocate, employ people with whom you get along well to assess pupil achievement in integrated schools). A study of policewomen's performance (Sichel, Note 4) that I ran in as objective a fashion as I knew how (and will tell you more about later) was suspected of being biased for and against police-women at the same time! Policemen were suspicious because the research team was staffed by females, and policewomen were equally suspicious because the research was sponsored and moni-tored by a police department they felt was opposed to women taking on patrol duties.

It would be naive of us to pretend we didn't have biases, and you, as experienced professionals working in a field, are sure to have formed many conclusions about which approaches are effec-tive, fair, humane, etc. Perhaps the best advice I can offer is that you make any relevant biases explicit to yourself and others before you even get involved in evaluation planning. If you believe that no counseling program for children can be successful unless it involves the children's parents, say so! Do you believe it so intensely that you couldn't give "children-only" programs fair study? Then turn over the responsibility for their evaluation to someone else. Do you have biases but think that by recognizing them you can give all programs objective evaluation? If you can couch your expectations in the form of meaningful guiding questions, and are prepared to bend over backward to compensate for your preconceptions, then fine! Evaluation research may well be worth bothering with in your organization.

Chapter 2

"BUT WE ALREADY KEEP STATISTICS!"

INFORMATION SYSTEMS VS. INFORMATIVE ANSWERS

There must be agencies that keep flawless statistics of immense use to them—places where cheerful and accessible gatekeepers dispense unerring statistical outpourings sufficient to answer all questions about program operations and impacts. If, however, there are such places, I don't know of them. The gap between having an information system at your agency and having it produce informative answers to your questions is likely to be a vast one, and the mechanisms needed for closing it are likely to be research strategies.

The basic problem may be the nature of the information you're routinely collecting. Unless this has been guided by some sort of plan or design, you're likely to have too much information and still not enough. A monthly computer listing of daily contacts between staff of a delinquency-prevention program and each of the program's clients may take up many pages of computer printout yet not provide any usable information beyond the average number of staff-client contacts taking place that month. It might be far more useful to know (in summary fashion) how many contacts took place with clients in each of three racial/ethnic groups, or how many of the monthly sessions were devoted to academic tutoring as opposed to counselling for personal problems.

Could your present information system give you data sufficient to answer any of the questions that may have occurred to you while you were reading the first chapter of this book—questions about program operations or about impact? Let's say you've opened a sobering-up station for alcoholics. You've been fortunate enough to get a contract with your city government so that it reimburses you with a fixed fee for each person spending a night in your facility. Naturally you've been concerned about your record keeping and have set up a small voucher-and-information system to enumerate clients served so that you can be reimbursed. But lo, an adjoining city has put a new wrinkle in your life! It has asked you to submit a proposal for setting up a similar facility for *it's* citizens. You sit down to write the proposal—you're full of enthusiasm! You begin to document your prior achievements. You look to your statistics and only then do you discover that all you know is how many client/nights you have provided. You have only a vague idea about average length of stay and number of repeated stays; you know nothing about how many clients also received welfare benefits. You don't even know much about them beyond the fact thay they're alcoholics. Your information system has let you down, but it has done so primarily because it was not built to do otherwise. It was not set up to answer a range of important questions about your program's operation. Designers of administrative record-keeping systems rarely think of evaluators who will come later.

Sometimes an information system has been planned with somewhat more forethought so that it has a capacity to generate useful answers. It may still not do so because the necessary linkages have not been set up. Beyond the crucial first link— setting up the system to provide the right kind of information— there are at least three kinds of links either necessary or helpful for translating information-system data into informative answers.

The most basic of these links is that of personnel. If your organization is large enough to have separate departments, those who generate the data are unlikely to be the same people who have need for it. In fact, there may be no real communication between those performing one and the other function. Merely issuing statistics out of one department and sending them to others through the internal mail is almost a guarantee that the statistics will never be tailored to actual current information needs. This problem is compounded when the data generators are computer experts who literally do not even speak the same language as organizational planners. It's often very hard for one to know what the other wants. For example, the data processing department in a hospital may be generating masses of data on outpatient clinic visits. Clinic staff may need data pertaining to patterns of clinic use by day of the week so that they can assign personnel most efficiently. Unless the units actually communicate with each other, there's likely to be lots of data from which no one can benefit. You may, if your problem is acute, need to designate a liaison person to make sure that people talk to each other!

A second kind of link between information-system data and information value is data analysis. Raw, undigested facts are rarely useful to planners and managers. Summary statistics are generally much more useful and should be built into the reports routinely generated by information-system personnel. Percentages, ranges, and averages are common tools for making raw data more manageable. Data can also be systematized by having the reports break down figures for subcategories of clients, services, or time periods. You may be getting quarterly census summaries from the computer, but what you really need to know is how stable your program attendance is from week to week during a given quarter. Or it might be a more detailed breakdown that would improve the information value of your routine data—for example, admissions on a weekly basis to each of the different services in your hospital. Or let's say you're administering a school district with more than one elementary school, and you've introduced a team-teaching arrangement in one third-grade class at each school. You want pupil achievement test scores broken out for you according to whether the children have been team taught or not and *also* which school they attended. Perhaps the students really benefited from the experience only in the school where a supportive principal gave special resources to his pet class.

A final kind of link between data and its use goes beyond communicating and systematizing. It's someone having responsibility for interpreting the data. Unless you, as a manager or planner, have a particular knack for looking at numbers and making sense out of them, you will probably find it extremely helpful to find someone who does this task well and to make sure he or she does it. Spotting trends or discontinuities, recognizing surprises in the data, gauging the importance of effects—all these can mean the difference between data that sit on your desk and data that help you plan and modify your organization's programs. Here's an example from my own experience.

I once finished analyzing a large, complex set of data from some research I had done. Being very close to that project for a long while, I was able to talk at great length about the numbers I had generated and the statistical details of my work. What I didn't realize at the time was that because I had gotten so close to the numbers, I no longer had perspective on what they meant. Getting real meaning and policy use from the data required collaboration with a colleague who was able to step back and interpret what I really had in hand. Now I know better, and perhaps so will you. Having statistics just doesn't automatically mean that you will have information!

Is Your Data Good Enough?

Even if you've got a genuinely useful information system and staff on hand to help you make use of it, the actual data in that system can still make or break its information value. If the data aren't accurate or dependable, neither will be the answers to your questions. Data that are accurate enough for rough operating feedback may be too "dirty" to be the basis for important decision making. Errors in recording data to go onto the system and errors in keypunching or transcribing data can make conclusions to be drawn from that data misleading. Incomplete sets of data are perhaps more common than inaccurate data. You may be missing data for key periods or sites, or you may be missing mainly those pieces of data that tell an unfavorable story about the program you're interested in evaluating. This is most likely to happen if program administrators supply the data to the information system. Selective reporting of data and a lot of procrastination in providing it are not unusual where people know that they are being monitored and especially if they feel that their jobs may depend on showing "good" statistics.

At this point it won't hurt to touch on two additional concepts that come from the research field. They both can be helpful in thinking about the quality of the data on your information system. The first is called *reliability*. The concept is close to the word's normal meaning—being reliable, consistent, and dependable. Data on which you're going to base decisions should be reproducible. They should not only be as error-free as possible, but they should be as circumstance-free as possible too. A given piece of data should be the same no matter who supplied it, on what day, and from which recording form. A good example is data on services that clients have been receiving. You should try to see that such data always comes from the most informed source as promptly as possible on record sheets with the same format. Changes in a recording system are one of the biggest problems in getting reliable data. You are likely to misattribute changes in sensitive indicators to your programs, when actually the changes come only from unreliability in data recording.

The other concept of possible relevance for your data's quality is *validity*. Validity refers basically to the extent to which you're measuring what you think you're measuring. Many items on information systems are stand-ins for broader phenomena. You may have test scores to measure client improvement. Especially if the tests are home grown, they may not have a close relationship with real improvement. Or you may have self-report data from questionnaires on things like drinking, smoking, or arrests. As Kinsey's sex studies taught us all a long time ago, there are ways to encourage people to give very frank answers about behavior of which they're not too proud (Kinsey, Note 5). But this isn't always easy, and your own data may be less valid than Kinsey's on homosexual activity and masturbation. You may have to go out and do a lot of solid interview work to get good data about sensitive topics.

And speaking of private kinds of things, you may have privacy issues to contend with if you try to use information-system data for purposes beyond client service. If the units of data on your information system are individual people, and they are identifiable by name or number, you might be on shaky ground if you use this data for purposes beyond strictly internal operational and administrative feedback.

The courts and federal agencies have become more and more involved in safeguarding the individual's right to privacy. There are elaborate sets of privacy guidelines and regulations that cover research conducted under federal grants (Note 6).

The best way to avoid potential problems in this area is to use individually identifiable data strictly for operating purposes on an as-needed basis, and to use data only in nonidentifiable summary form for statistical and research use. There is rarely any necessity for names at all; identifying numbers are needed more often, so that relationships between individual characteristics and program features can be assessed or in order to trace individuals' patterns over time. This can be handled by keeping the list of name and number equivalencies restricted to one or two staff members. And, of course, nothing should be circulated in any document that could be connected to a particular individual. Remember that if you're reporting on an "anonymous" group of a few clients, any clues to their characteristics are likely to give away who they are.

POTENTIAL FOR EVALUATIONS USING INFORMATION SYSTEMS

After all these sour notes about research using information systems, I'd like to cheer you up a bit. As you suspected to begin with, that expensive statistics-generating information system you already have might be able to do some evaluation work for you yet.

If you can arrange to solve the problems I've been discussing and can come up with a plan to use your information system to answer specific questions, you should be able to make it work for you. In summary, you will enhance your chances of getting useful data from your information system by:

- knowing what questions you want answers to
- planning the information gathering to provide the answers you need
- making sure communication occurs between yourself (or other planners) and data handlers
- getting the data reported in a usable fashion
- having someone who can interpret what the data mean
- ensuring that the data are as accurate as possible, as well as reliable and valid
- seeing to it that you protect individuals' privacy in your data handling

The ideal way to make an information system serve research needs as well as operating ones is to design the dual capacities into the original system. Such a design was done for the mini-bus system for elderly and disabled people that I referred to earlier. An information system was created so that it would be able to provide operational feedback and verification of services provided, *plus* extensive research information about patterns of system use and characteristics of the clients. It could not only tell you how many trips had been taken by wheelchair-ridden passengers but even tell you what destinations these clients had gone to and how the destinations differed from those of ambulatory clients.

Especially if your evaluation questions concern program operation, you may be able to make good use of the figures you're already getting in routine reports from your existing information system. A common research comparison is between program data and "baseline" data—that is, data from a period prior to the program. You may have data of this type already in your files. If your information system can generate data for an earlier period in the same form as that for the program period, then you may have the basis for an evaluation that can be conducted very simply out of your own information system.

If you have data that is available in a continuous series starting before programs or innovations and continuing through the program period, you can take advantage of this storehouse. Social scientists have recently become enamored with what are called *time-series analyses*. This means that data from a series of points in time are examined for changes that occur in conjunction with program or system changes. For example, the British government had data on traffic fatalities that existed in an uninterrupted series for many years. When they instituted a "breathalyser" program for testing and getting drunk drivers off the road, it was reasoned that if the program was successful, the number of traffic fatalities ought to go down. They were able to use the ongoing time-series data on fatalities to demonstrate that a decrease in fatalities (which was greater than normal year-to-year fluctuations) had indeed occurred right after the institution of the program against drunk drivers (Ross, et al., Note 7). In Connecticut the technique was used to assess the effect of a state-police crackdown on over-the-speed-limit driving (Campbell & Ross, Note 8). Time-series data on traffic accidents were examined for a discontinuous decrease following the crackdown. And in New York State several criminal-justice statistics available in a time-series have been used to gauge the effects of a change in the law concerning narcotics offenders (Note 9). If your organization either generates or has access to time-series data, perhaps you too would find it responsive to changes in your programs or methods, and useful for their evaluation.

Even in the absence of lengthy historical data sets, you may have a broad enough data base to look at the interrelationship among a number of program factors and indicators at one or several points in time. For example, the Prosecutor's Management Information System (PROMIS) has become an integral part of many district attorneys' operations in major cities of the U.S. The extensive data base that is accumulated through this system lends itself well to research of a "correlational" nature (relating various factors to each other). In fact, a large number of research reports have already resulted from an analysis of data from the Washington, D.C., PROMIS system (Note 10).

If you had a PROMIS system that gave you information on each criminal case being prosecuted in your city, you might be able to use it to find out whether you were really able to prosecute auto thefts from start to finish within one month in your new anti-auto-theft program. You might want to use your system to find out whether defendants with prior criminal records were receiving heavier prison sentences. You may be able to make use of your own large data base to look at the relationship of program factors and nonprogram factors to certain outcomes. For example, are women who complete our program able to get jobs? There are many data analytic techniques, such as multiple-regression (Note 11), that are specially suited to looking at interplays of factors, and you might want to have the services of someone versed in them.

You may be able to reprogram or modify an existing information system to yield evaluation information too. Sometimes it is the items of information being collected and summarized that need modifying, and it can really be quite easy. For example, you may already keep a file of names and addresses of those who have donated money to your charitable organization, but need additional demographic information to prepare a profile of your contributors. By adding several items to your donation forms and seeing to it that the information is put onto the computer system, you can obtain much more useful output to tell you something about those most likely to support your organization.

For some agencies, the right information is already being collected but it is not being provided in a usable report format. You may be receiving information at too fine a level *or* too global a level. You may be getting information too frequently or not often enough. You may need breakdowns of the information into useful categories. Or you may know only that the present reporting setup doesn't fill your needs but are unsure as to what would be better.

Perhaps, as you read on through this book, you'll have some new insights about how to get evaluation "payoffs" from your information system data. And you may also decide to go beyond the limits of these systems for at least some of your evaluation needs.

Chapter 3

REINVENTING THE WHEEL— HOW TO AVOID IT

Before you plunge into any evaluation work, you should make sure that you're not "reinventing the wheel." Surprisingly, many people doing research ignore this whole issue. Whatever time and effort you devote to looking for existing data and methodology is likely to be well spent. In this chapter I will make a number of suggestions as to where to look. The looking will be up to you!

CHECK OUT PRIOR STUDIES IN THE "ANNALS" OF YOUR AGENCY

Perhaps your agency has conducted research in the past. If the questions involved were similar to those you face now, you may have an ideal historical data base that can be built upon and updated. It's helpful to ask old-timers about this. There may be gold in the personal files of people who have been around your place for a while. Be alert for early evaluation reports that are in draft or memo form, since studies that few people know about probably didn't get written up for the world in a formal report.

They may even (horrors!) have been suppressed—as was an important study with which I am acquainted.

In this case it was a study of policewomen that was suppressed by the leadership of a major metropolitan police department. There was a great deal to be learned from the study—both by policy makers and also by researchers planning new work in this area. But it was held back from release, supposedly because the small size of the group studied made any conclusions too tentative (Greenwald & Connolly, Note 12).

Studies may have been done *about* your organization by an oversight body. Perhaps your agency was one among several that were reviewed in a report to your mayor or in a cross-city comparison. Frequently such reports are concerned with budgets and expenditures. If you can locate this kind of material, it's apt to be very helpful for planning a study of your own that involves cost analysis.

So may management consultant reports. These reports may be particularly useful for baseline information on organizational factors, morale, staffing, and productivity. Especially if your current research questions relate mainly to operations rather than impact, knowing something about what has already been looked at in your organization may save you considerable duplication of effort. You may even want to include all or part of such prior reports (duly credited, of course) as part of your present research proposals and write-ups.

Even if an old review you unearth wasn't called a study, maybe it contains dependable historical data or suggests useful ways to investigate your questions. In-house memoranda in old files may have material of this sort. You may find fragments of data in your agency's old files that may be useful to you as baseline information or as a reality test for the planning of new research. There may be clues as to why prior studies that were attempted never came to successful conclusions. Perhaps the kind and amount of data to be collected was too ambitious, or perhaps it was too prone to error; or it could be that the problem was (and still is) forcing a study into a single dimension. This was the case with a notorious study done before my time for one of my employers (Fishman, Note 13). Massive amounts of criminal-justice system data from a great number of sources were pushed and shoved in an effort to fit them into a pre-set research design. Almost a million dollars later, the funding agencies had to admit that the entire enterprise had been sadly impractical and unsuccessful. I hope that everyone can learn something from the experience that will save them similar grief in the future.

FIND OUT WHAT OTHER AGENCIES HAVE DONE

An excellent way of benefiting from others' prior efforts is to look at various organizations that grapple with problems similar to yours. In the private sector this may amount to espionage, but for public and nonprofit groups—whether they're similar agencies in different towns, or agencies with slightly different responsibilities in your own town or state—chances are they'll be willing to share some of their experiences and written material with you. Sometimes you discover something of potential use in an offhand way: while working on a study of certain prosecution projects, one of my staff members mentioned that his previous employer had done a small study of a couple of the same projects. Other times you have to do some digging yourself.

You may be able to get access to potentially useful computerized data bases maintained by private or government organizations. For example, federal government agencies have computerized files on drug and alcohol abuse, major-crime statistics and employment (to name just a few). State agencies frequently maintain data bases on education and health. Nonprofit survey research corporations have data banks covering public opinion on an enormous range of topics (Note 14). While access to all these sources is limited, legitimate public and nonprofit agencies can frequently make use of them for nominal charges. You may find that they contain enough data of the right sort to answer your research questions without your doing any data collection on your own. Or you may find that many, if not all, of your concerns have already been examined.

Additional data bases may enhance your ability to use your own information system for doing program evaluations. As I discussed in the previous chapter, it is important to have some basis for comparison in evaluating the meaning of the figures that your system is generating. A data base from another agency may be suitable for this purpose. For example, you may be producing data on the school attendance of adolescent boys in your town. This information is much more useful if you have something to compare it with. If you maintain the same figures from a number of years in the past and can make internal comparisons, that is useful. But a comparison of particular benefit could be with adolescent boys in other localities. Finding and gaining access to such data that other places have assembled can save you the burden of collecting this data yourself, and can keep the scope of your own evaluation work more reasonable.

JOIN UP WITH COMPLEMENTARY GROUPS

Sometimes it is possible to work out marriages (or at least temporary affairs) of convenience between your agency and another or others. This can save you considerable groping in the dark (ha ha!).

One possibility is to become involved in a joint planning venture that could lead to a future research project. You would want to choose for this collaboration an organization having experience and skills that complement those of your own. For example, a university group interested in studying police patrol innovations invited their city's police department to enter into a joint weekly seminar with them (Note 15). What the academic people lacked in substantive knowledge was to be furnished by the police department; the police would gain the university's analytic and research expertise. The arrangement worked out only moderately well, perhaps because the police did not feel they were gaining enough. The joint planning approach seems most promising with agencies that have equally good reason to be involved.

When a problem is particularly pressing to a number of groups, then an action/research consortium can be formed. This can be extremely valuable for contributing various kinds of expertise to a problem area. I have had personal experience with one such group set up by an outside coordinator to experiment with a new approach to fighting arson in a major urban county (Note 16). The constituent agencies of fire department, police department, and district attorney had a history of mutual distrust and resentment. They had much initial difficulty in working with each other, but certainly each acquired considerable knowledge about arson that they hadn't previously possessed. Some of this knowledge is now being applied to further initiatives by the coordinating body.

Take Advantage of Publications, Reports, and Computer Programs

Books, monographs, and articles may be extremely useful to you in beginning your own research. They can suggest guiding questions, provide actual data forms or questionnaires, shape appropriate types of data to collect, and tell you about problems. There may be so many problems with collecting a certain type of data that you probably shouldn't collect it. Other kinds of data have typical patterns that limit the statistics you can use with them. Knowing about problems ahead of time can save you much trouble on the other end!

Finding good sources may be relatively easy. Many fields of interest have bibliographies, abstracts of articles, and reference lists and services. A recent innovation has been the use of the computer to search for and retrieve the titles of documents related to particular topic areas.

You may want to get somewhat far afield from your primary area in order to find helpful material. A recent study I completed was funded by an agency that required an extensive literature review of our problem area (Note 17). The agency suggested books that seemed only tangentially related and, while it was generally not worth the additional labor, we did find some pertinent material somewhat removed from our immediate area.

If you're planning to make use of computer programs in your research, there are reference sources that list existing programs. Computer hardware vendors would know about these. "Canned" programs can certainly help you avoid a great deal of programming expense and effort. One of the most widely known and useful "packages" of such programs for research is "SPSS," Statistical Package for the Social Sciences, which can be obtained from the University of Chicago. Writing just one of the subroutines available within this package could take a person doing it on their own huge amounts of labor and time—and even then, one's own computer programs don't always work too well!

GET EXPERIENCE ON YOUR TEAM

Treating your staff to a "learning experience" may be great for employee morale, but the person-hours spent while they acquaint themselves with substance and methodology can be avoided by getting some existing talent going for you. One of the best ways to do this is to hire it. Recruiting staff who have been involved in successful evaluation work similar to what you're contemplating is ideal. You may be able to find such people through ads in the trade periodicals and newsletters. Then they can bring you both substantive and methodological background. Settling for methodological talent is easy because the schools are turning out a glut of social scientists, but you're apt to find yourself back at that old wheel. A number of prestigious companies find themselves in this position because they hire marvelously bright novices from marvelously good schools. Such people are often creative at problem solving and are usually able to learn quickly. But if quickly in your field means six months, then you are the one who must judge the wisdom of the investment.

There's one kind of experience you can buy that I'd like to caution you about in particular. A social scientist who has done laboratory-type research in your problem area probably isn't going to save you any learning pains. For example, a psychologist whose prior career was devoted to studying the physiological effects of methadone on rats is not likely to be an asset to your evaluation of a methadone-maintenance program for welfare mothers. The problems and talents required in doing research in the real world—the "field," as it is called—are extremely different from an academic setting, and success in one is no guarantee of anything in the other.

Chapter 4

BALLPARK EVALUATION PLANNING
YOU CAN DO

Even if you've never studied research nor been through an evaluation, your common sense may be the most valuable evaluation planning tool at your agency.

LET THE NATURE OF YOUR QUESTIONS DEFINE A FOCUS

Just as you would tailor the shape of a new action program to what you believed the need to be, so should you tailor its evaluation. If you need to answer questions about the physical performance of police officers, you should deliberately shape your research to concentrate there rather than elsewhere. While this seems obvious, let us never take the value of common sense for granted. For every study that has really focused on an agreed-upon problem area, there has probably been another that hasn't. It's wise to focus your organization's efforts somewhat specifically right from the start, and to go afield only when you plan to. Otherwise, what's easiest to study tends to be what gets studied. In the example of studying police officers' physical performance, if you post observers to watch the police, you find that they rarely do anything physically strenuous. It's a lot easier to assess how they talk to citizens, because they do that a lot more. And lo, the evaluation of police physical performance can turn into a study that won't really provide answers in that area at all!

LET THE NATURE OF YOUR QUESTIONS DICTATE THE SCOPE OF YOUR RESEARCH

This is perhaps the trickiest part of research planning. How big should your research effort be? This is again a matter of common sense, although there are some guidelines from the experience of others that could be helpful to you.

Questions that relate to operations tend to need less extensive research than those relating to impact. Feedback that will help fine-tune a program can usually be gotten from short-term, limited kind of research. Definitive evaluations of impact are almost always bigger efforts. They usually occur after programs have been established for a while and have settled down into a stable pattern. If major policy decisions will be guided by the impact evaluation's results, then the evaluation is probably going to be quite major.

In fact, the degree of conclusiveness you need from your findings can be used as a rule of thumb to guide scope. The more conclusive and dependable (rather than suggestive) your answers must be, the more elaborate the research likely to be needed.

However, it's my impression that we tend to do things too ambitiously at first and to overestimate the definitiveness we need. It's often sufficient to settle for less dependable answers, at least in your first research foray into a particular area. The results of relatively small evaluation studies will probably be conclusive enough to make decisions and changes on the basis of their findings. "Quick and dirty" studies, which may be sketchily planned, involve little resource investment, and operate mainly by seat-of-the-pants methods, are sometimes sufficient too. Getting your data from one of the secondary sources discussed in the previous chapter can also save you lots of time and money. While secondary data might not be as extensive or reliable as data you collected yourself, you can use it to draw qualified conclusions, which may be quite enough! I'll give you an example of a corner-cutting procedure that I used recently.

A large study on district attorneys that I was conducting had been laid out carefully and well in advance of collecting data in the field. But an important new research question emerged. What should we do? Go ahead with research as planned and ignore the new question? Or try to add on the additional labor and time necessary to investigate it? The solution we took was a compromise. We decided to alter some of the research methods we were using so that we could distribute our existing resources to study the new question. We had been going through the original files on criminal cases in many jurisdictions, an information-rich source, but a highly time-consuming operation. Our change in method involved finding and using summary log books rather than original files in one major jurisdiction. This freed up the necessary resources to study the new question and still allowed us to answer our original questions, with only a little information sacrificed.

MATTERS OF TIMING

Your time frame should also be an important factor in shaping the research you'll be doing. If you need answers quickly, you shouldn't be planning a year-long study. If you'll be trying to get research funding from an outside source (something I'll be talking more about in Chapter 6), this will take time in itself, and delay your eventual startup. In fact, if there is any general guideline about the timing of evaluation studies, it is that everything takes longer than you think it will. If you're in a hurry, you should probably limit your evaluation work to a very simple investigation of one, or at most two, research issues. If that goes well and is completed close to your schedule, you can go on and do more.

Could you imagine getting to the end of a long evaluation study and discovering that people no longer care about the questions or problems it was set up to investigate? They have moved on to new concerns (or to new program fads) and you are left to search among your findings for kernels of relevance to current problems and programs. I found myself in that position once, but it won't happen to me again because I will try to look "down the road" intelligently to deliberately plan research time frames that are appropriate to what I see. I recommend you do the same with your good judgment!

Guessing About Methods

It's usually helpful to have some tentative ideas about the methods you'll use. You can make changes later, but you should be able to talk about a study of one sort or the other when you go to look for support within your own organization, or to locate "experts" or funding.

Some kinds of research questions suggest particular methods. For example, questions about employee morale are almost always studied by asking the employees how they feel—using either an interview or a questionnaire. And questions about the prevalence of a given social phenomenon such as unemployment or crime are usually studied through officially produced statistics.

This is not to say that your best choice of method is always obvious from the start. For example, you may get a more accurate picture of employee morale by using an indirect measure, such as employee attendance, which has previously been shown to be related to morale. You could look at personnel records for lateness and "days-taken-off" by the group under study and compare them with the records of other employees. And to assess the volume and nature of crime it may be misleading to head simply for the official crime statistics. In fact, recent studies have gotten a more reliable picture of crime by surveying citizens about criminal incidents that have happened to them. This has meant concentrating this kind of research on law-abiding citizens rather than criminals! Some imagination can help your common sense in identifying the best focus for your research.

Don't feel that you must always choose one from among alternate methods of studying the same thing. While it is expensive, it is frequently wise to employ two or more methods to address the same questions. Weaknesses in each method will be compensated; and if findings are similar, your level of confidence in them will be that much greater.

You will be able to exclude some methods fairly easily because they are not suited to your probable scope or time frame. Or certain methods may recommend themselves because of convenience or prior experience at your agency. But, above all, your research questions should determine the methodological direction you head off in.

SOME REPRESENTATIVE "BALLPARKS"

1. *Collecting a Bit of Information:*   When you want feedback quickly about a program that you may want to modify, you won't want to plan anything long-term or elaborate. The most direct methods are probably the best—asking staff or clients about their perceptions of your program and/or gathering simple numerical indicators of how the program is working.

    Basically you would be able to carry out this kind of effort with no particular experience and no expert assistance. It's likely to be the kind of thing your organization is used to doing on an informal basis, but has never thought of as evaluation work.

2. *Tapping Into Your Agency's Information System:* When your research questions need quantitative answers, sometimes this is a highly efficient way to get information for evaluation purposes. As Chapter 2 suggested, you may be able to use or modify your existing information system to provide evaluative data to answer present and future research questions. You may

need a computer expert but, even then, the scope of the work is likely to be manageable within a small budget and time frame. And the improvements in information that the system can provide are likely to repay you as a management benefit well into the future.

3. *Getting Large Amounts of Data at Low Cost:* This kind of "ballpark" is a particular favorite of mine because it offers a challenge to ingenuity. Sometimes you can find summaries of large amounts of data that are reliable enough to use. Or you may be able to invent a way to collect a lot of data so that it becomes a stream-lined process. Often there are as many possibilities as there are creative minds put to the planning, so that expenses and time can still be kept low.

4. *Doing a Large Study in Phases:* Sometimes you can break down your research questions so that you answer some before others. Or if you need a very detailed answer to one or two questions, perhaps you can begin with a strategy able to provide only a bare-bones answer and then to build upon that later, as time, money, and interest dictate. For example, you might begin by consulting secondary data sources like reports and books, and only later go on to collect your own data.

5. *When Only the Most Rigorous, Extensive Work Will Do:* Sometimes you will know you want or need a large study. If this is true, you should allow an ample planning period as well as adequate resources for data collection and analysis of all sorts. You could be interviewing people or observing project operations or going through source records—or combinations of all these and more. This kind of ballpark tends to get crowded with professionals and the need for outside money. And it's these two topics that you'll be reading about in the next two chapters, to help you decide whether and how much of them you may need.

Chapter 5

SHOULD YOU CALL IN THE EXPERTS?

Will you make terrible errors if you decide to go it alone? Probably not—but even if you do, the repercussions of drawing incorrect conclusions are likely to be limited. In my experience, you often have a chance to try again if your first strategy didn't pan out. But there still may be stages, especially in a large study, when you want help with your evaluation work. There are basically four possibilities: help with thinking, with doing, with analyzing, and with report writing. Naturally, you could have any combination you like, as well.

GETTING HELP WITH YOUR EVALUATION THINKING

This may really be the stage where some expertise is most likely to pay off. The right Someone may be able to alert you to what is feasible as an evaluation strategy and what is not. He or she may know that the idea you have has been tried unsuccessfully elsewhere, or that it needed something additional to succeed. An expert may be able to lay out several options for you to choose among, tell you what each is likely to involve in personnel and costs, and otherwise suggest intriguing ideas. I'm a social psychologist and not an architect. When architects come to my house, they're able to see remodeling possibilities I never imagine. Then I can decide whether I want to go ahead or not, doing the work myself or using a contractor.

A wonderful way that an expert may help you during the thinking/planning period is by writing a proposal for grant funds to do the evaluation. If you've chosen somebody who's good at this, you could wind up with both good ideas and the money with which to implement them.

HAVING THE EXPERTS COLLECT YOUR DATA

Generally you wouldn't bring anyone in to do this unless you were getting help all the way along. But occasionally you need a specialist in the kind of data collection you've chosen. Survey methodology is the best example of this. Where there is to be a large scale survey of the public, it's likely to be done better and at lower cost by those who know the business. And there are so many problems with getting truthful and complete information in surveys that it is often a relief to put it in other hands.

HELP WITH THE NUMBERS

Many evaluators, even experts themselves, call on statistics and data-processing experts to make sense out of the data they've collected. You may want to do this too, especially if you have large amounts of data that can't be tabulated by hand.

Another specialist often needed is a person who can prepare realistic research budgets. Look for a record of successful experience.

Do You Need a Writer?

This kind of need certainly isn't limited to evaluations; but if your evaluation report will be widely distributed, you may want to go beyond your staff's writing talents. Poorly presented results can do a great disservice to a substantial evaluation effort. And well-presented ones can argue cogently for what you believe the data suggest.

Eenie, Meenie . . .

Who is likely to be the right kind of expert for you? Under certain circumstances you may contract a whole evaluation out to a consulting firm or a university research group. Or you may hire an individual "consultant" to perform or oversee all or part of your evaluation work.

In any event, if you are planning on any kind of help, see more than one "expert" before you decide who the helper should be. Some helpers are going to be a lot more helpful than others, and may even cost you the least in the long run!

If your evaluation will address questions that are primarily operational or management oriented, you will probably want to consider management consultants. They tend to be prompt and deadline oriented. Unfortunately, they also tend to use "boiler-plate" formats and try to fit your work into their standard routine, rather than paying attention to your own research questions. Look for those with a specialty in your area who can show you reports or other products that they've done. Try to talk with some other agency for whom they've worked. As in many areas of life, prior performance is a useful predictor in the absence of prescience! If your research questions are geared to costs and benefits, you will want to be sure you're buying this kind of expertise. You will also want to be sure that you are getting a firm with a good reputation, which doesn't just "knock off" their evaluations with a weather eye to the profit margin. And, if at all possible, you should avoid "political" choices that are really not going to do a good job for you. It's also best to select a local firm so that they won't have a good excuse for staying away from your program, and you won't be paying travel costs every time they do show up.

Social scientists are the other general kind of consultant you may want to consider. These are people who have been trained in a university to do research. They represent an enormous range of specialties and abilities. There are economists, sociologists, psychologists, social psychologists, organizational experts, behavioral scientists . . . and the list goes on! Some have had experience mainly of a theoretical nature; others have studied problems in laboratory settings lacking the complexity of the real world. You should look for people who have "applied" research experience, meaning that they have been studying problems in natural settings, and, one hopes, dealing with complex social factors. You want research that is "applied" to your specific questions rather than being "basic" research to advance general knowledge in a scholarly field.

You should not assume that because an individual is affiliated with a college or university that he or she is necessarily very talented. Many are, but some aren't. Generally, university-sponsored research institutes are staffed with capable people, but again this shouldn't be assumed without some other corroboration. As with management consultants, I think the best way to evaluate potential evaluators is to look at something they've already done. Is it on your wave length? Can you understand what they've written? Do they seem to have focused on important areas or does their work seem trivial? Some advantages of using university folks is that they may offer their services at low cost in return for access to your organization. And they may provide free student assistants and computer resources. But they all go away for three months in the summer, and while most of us would like to do the same, we settle for the end of August and often need work done in June and July!

Perhaps you can ask for and get a concept paper on your own evaluation problem from one or two prospective consultants. In this way, you can get a better idea of a number of things: whether they already possess a sufficient knowledge base to grapple intelligently with your issues; whether they seem to think in practical terms and to be geared to real-life settings; and to get clues to their methodological preferences to see if that is what you want.

Some academic people only want to work with numbers and records—they call it "hard data." This kind of data may or may not be the best kind to inform your evaluation questions. I had a work colleague who always wanted to apply a particular statistical technique to his research work. This technique was perfectly useful in its place, but its place wasn't all of those he wanted to use it in! Other researchers have a "softer" focus; they stress interviewing or observing. Again, this may or may not be appropriate.

You should probably be looking for more methodological flexibility if you're calling someone in for the evaluation planning stage. That way, your expert's specialties won't be that much of a constraint on your evaluation design. You're unlikely to be very interested in "communication nets," but the anthropologist you hire may (like one I know) specialize in studying them, and may be hoping your evaluation can be the basis for a magnum opus in the "Journal of Communication Nets" (actually a fictitious title, but true in spirit!). You want to make sure that the people you select are both prepared for and interested in the frequently mundane evaluation needs of a functioning work setting. If you decide that you need outside help at one or several stages of your evaluation efforts, you should be sure that your practical needs are always placed first. When this fails to happen, the work is never what you had in mind.

OUTSIDERS SHOULD BECOME HONORARY INSIDERS

In fact, an outsider will need not just to become acquainted, but more likely to immerse himself (or herself) in your organization in order to know how to help you.

You should insist that your "expert" also become expert on

your particular agency characteristics and problems. Even if it will take your staff's time to accomplish this, it is essential in my opinion that your outsider not stay on the outside. Your staff may argue that it is disruptive to have an outside evaluator participate in ongoing activities. Sometimes it is. If you've chosen well, the person will undoubtedly ask questions, poke around a bit, and be a bit of a nuisance. But make sure that an official welcome mat is out and publicized, that evaluators receive an escort when they want one and are left on their own when they don't. Don't forget to advise them about and issue invitations to significant meetings and events. Your evaluator may not be thrilled to be in attendance as often as this, but you should insist on it, preferably in your contract.

CONTRACTING FOR THE WORK

Having a written contract with any outside evaluator is very important because if you construct it properly, it will protect you. You should probably have it drawn up by a lawyer for your organization. Depending on how your local situation works, you may have to issue some sort of solicitation for bids before you can proceed to a contract with a particular outside evaluator. This could be in the form of a formal "RFP" or "RFC" (request for proposals or request for contracts).

You can make this quite specific although if you're looking for planning help, it could be difficult. In any event, you can specify your major evaluation questions, the general ballpark of your study in terms of scope, time frame and probable methodology. You will probably also have to mention an upper dollar figure, something I'll be telling you about how to estimate in the next chapter.

After you've chosen your expert and are drawing up a contract, there are a number of things you'll want to put into it. First, you'll want to hold your expert to your time frame, so all deadlines should be made explicit. This functions as protection when it is backed up with knowledge that funds will be withheld if specific products are not delivered on time. The products that you expect should also be detailed in the contract. If you want to have an "executive summary" as well as (or in lieu of) a highly technical final report, the contract is the place to say so. If you want an oral presentation of findings, that should be stipulated. The more accountability you can build in, the better. You might want to insist on extensive documentation of all phases of the work— plans, interim findings, data summaries. In this fashion you won't be left dependent on your expert if your funds run out or if you want to terminate the arrangement. At least one administrator could tell a horror story of being left "high and dry" when his expert departed without leaving a codebook to make sense out of a computer data analysis. If you insist on putting *everything* in writing, however, you may be running up a large expenditure for your expert's time without substantial benefit to you. Your own judgment is probably the best guide in this regard.

Despite the fact that your expert looked wonderful when you selected him or her, the bloom may pale at a later date and you may want to get out of the arrangement. Here, again, a well-drawn contract will protect you by specifying the conditions under which the arrangement can be terminated. These conditions can include failure to deliver products in a timely fashion, failure to respond to your agency's specific research questions, failure to be present at your agency for some stipulated minimum amount of time, failure to satisfactorily present and interpret evaluation findings, etc.

THE IN-HOUSE ALTERNATIVE

You may decide that you don't really want or need outside help. You might have felt this all along, or come to this conclusion after a couple of scary meetings with research heavyweights who both intimidated you and appeared to be expensive! What are your chances of getting satisfactory results on your own? Will you be able to plan and execute a useful evaluation study on your own steam (or with a little help from books and materials like this one)?

It will depend on a number of factors, and you should probably weigh them in a fairly systematic fashion before committing yourself to a wholly in-house route.

First, you will want to consider whether the purpose of the evaluation will be well served by an in-house study. Generally, research questions relating to operations can suitably be answered by in-house research. Your own staff will be most familiar with program operations and will be in an excellent position to suggest refinements based on simple, short-term data collection and analysis. For exmaple, if you were running a jail where security had become unsatisfactory to the community, you might want do an in-house study of your security arrangements such as off-limit areas and visitors' reception procedures. In fact, in such a case initiating an in-house evaluation might forestall some kind of unwelcome official investigation, and might result in real improvements to your agency's functioning.

Questions about program impact or cost-effectiveness can also be handled by in-house research, but in this case ability and credibility become concerns. If the scope of the study is to be large, you may not have sufficient staff to handle it on your own, and the staff may not possess the requisite skills. Also, your findings may be hard to defend to others who challenge your objectivity (even assuming you have been objective). It is this type of study that is usually performed by an independent contractor, often commissioned by an oversight body.

Apart from the purpose of your study, practical factors will also bear on whether you choose to do it in-house. By way of example: your staff may not have time to collect data; you may suspect or fear a tendency to falsify data; you may have a time frame that won't permit even the delay involved to select an evaluator and develop a contract; you may have your own research staff to keep busy (and they may be quite good); there may be funding to do a "sociological" study when no one on your staff even knows what this means; etc., etc.

If you do plan to do an in-house study, you may want to add to your present staff to do it. It may be in your interest to build up a capable in-house staff for ongoing research and evaluation work. On the other hand, while you may have greater control of "resident experts," it may be no cheaper than bringing in a consulting firm with its own people. You won't have to give consultants paid vacations or jolly them along or take care of them when the study is over; and it usually takes a long period of careful looking to assemble a high-quality permanent staff, especially in public agencies where civil-service constraints and low salaries make it hard to attract high-caliber people. You may want to experiment with a combination of in-house staff and outside consultants to give you some of the advantages of both arrangements.

In-house studies should be kept reasonably separate from other ongoing operations. Otherwise your researchers are likely to be hopelessly compromised, and your organization's management may get poor information. At least one social reform organization (Vera Institute, Note 18) has done many in-house impact evaluations successfully by having a separate research department staffed by professionals who insist on the department's integrity. Having a separate research staff to collect data is very useful; data collected by harried program staff (even if they have no ulterior motives) may be inaccurate and incomplete. If data collection is left to program people, they should know they will be monitored, and research staff should verify a sample of the data.

Incidentally, whether or not program staff collect data, it is particularly important to get them involved in the study in a positive way. Otherwise you may be generating administrative headaches out of proportion to the potential usefulness of your research.

In-house studies have the unfortunate tendency to be more casually handled than studies that involve outsiders. You may want to try to structure the in-house work so that everyone takes it as seriously as they should. This could involve requiring progress reports or presentations from the researchers, and it might be helpful to establish benchmark points at which certain stages of the evaluation are expected to be completed. The in-house route may work best when you pool resources with some other agency to do a joint evaluation; agency pride tends to surface and bring out best-foot-forward performance from both staffs.

Books like this may furnish some assistance with an in-house evaluation. But alas, you shouldn't expect too much! Your research questions and needs, while probably not unique, will have their own wrinkles. And those may not be the same wrinkles your author has chosen to iron out. He or she certainly won't have covered all of them.

Look for additional free help from foundations or reference services. But if you decide you need outside help, it is likely that you'll have to pay for it. And now—how much might it cost? Read on!

Chapter 6

WHAT SHOULD IT COST AND WHO WILL PAY?

Budgeting for evaluation research is really a process of informed guessing, where you try to be right more often than wrong. If you hire outside experts, it's going to cost more in general. But doing it in-house or out, expenditures will generally be proportional to the scope of the study—the bigger, the more expensive.

THE MAJOR COSTS

Personnel will be your largest expense, dependent, of course, on the number of people who will be working on the evaluation. The "price" of researchers varies widely, however, and all kinds of salary combinations and bottom-line figures are possible. Generally you will need: one research administrator who will supervise the activities; someone (it could be the same person) who will accomplish the data analysis, interpret the findings, and present the results; and data collectors. Data collectors need not be a large personnel expense. Sometimes they can be drawn from program staff, and even if specially hired, they rarely need to possess specialized skills. An exception to this general rule is when you will be doing interviewing of a complicated nature to collect your information. In this case you will probably need to (and want to) pay a premium to get experienced interviewers. If you hired them yourself you would pay them on an hourly basis—perhaps $7 or so per hour in the New York area in 1980. Travel expenses also have to be reimbursed. Paying by the interview can lead to all kinds of chicanery—you should avoid it!

Research managers and analysts will cost you a good bit more than data collectors, but we are really not a highly paid lot! Chances are that even if you are a raise-overdue public manager, you're making more money than an average research project director. In most parts of the country in 1980, $25,000 per year buys the full-time services of a competent research chief with considerable experience. If the scope of your intended work is small, then you may not even need such a person full time, and almost surely not for a full year. The same is true of data analysts or statisticians. These people's annual salaries rarely exceed $20,000, although people with substantial computer skills are naming their own price these days!

When you're dealing with an outside consulting organization, personnel costs are included in the figures quoted to you; it's important to ask whose services you'll have, and for how much of their time. Some consulting firms will hire people especially for your job, but they may be very junior folks of the kind you could hire directly for a lot less. (However, if the group's guiding star is really going to give them a lot of guidance, then the personnel package may be right for you.) Another cost caution about consultants is that if they're not local people, you will have to reimburse them for their travel time and expenses to get to your site. This can run into a very large expense.

There are some insidious hidden costs associated with having outside groups do your research. University groups and foundations often charge "indirect costs"—over and above actual research costs—to cover some of their general operating expenses.

The percentage ranges widely, but for some groups it exceeds 100%, and you may be paying $50,000 to get a $25,000 study! Management consultants calculate a profit margin rather than an overhead rate, but it may be all the same to your budget because this is also likely to reduce the value in work that you receive.

Data processing can be another major expense of evaluation work. If you are going to be analyzing computerized data, you may have to pay for keypunching and verifying, programming, data handling, and "running" time. These can be substantial costs that may rival your personnel ones in magnitude, depending on your volume of data and what you want to do with it. When the money is coming from your group's budget, you're likely to be particularly sensitive to keeping down costs. And even when you expect to be working with grant funds, you're unlikely to be comfortable with profligacy! There are a number of ways to save evaluation dollars. Some of them you're likely to learn only after you've spent and regretted it. Others can be anticipated.

GETTING GOOD PEOPLE FOR LESS MONEY

For example, personnel costs can be shaved in a number of ways. It is often possible to stagger the introduction and termination of personnel. People working on evaluation planning obviously come first, data-collection and analysis personnel at varying later stages. Data collectors and analysts may actually only be needed for a brief period and this can reduce costs considerably. Sometimes these people can move from one evaluation project to another as the need for their kind of service peaks and wanes. Also, it is often sufficient to share key people with other projects. You may be able to pay a research supervisor for only one day each week. You will, of course, have to judge whether you will be sacrificing something important by doing this or perhaps delaying the progress of the evaluation. You may have had experiences with part-timers that color the way you feel about using them. My experiences have been good. I think that three-day-a-weekers often produce as much as full-timers, particularly if the press of work is not steady. Also part-time arrangements may allow you to hire young mothers with professional training who are often highly motivated to excel at their "re-entry" jobs. Your conscience should ensure that you don't take undue advantage of their usual willingness to work for low wages.

Students can also be hired for evaluation work, and they are frequently cost-saving and satisfactory staff members. In my experience their biggest drawback is that they need a great deal of supervision. The best among them are graduate students who are ready to function professionally on their own. There is a strong temptation to turn over whole evaluations to this relatively inexpensive kind of "expert." But lack of real-world experience typifies these young people even more than more seasoned academic experts, and you may not get even your reduced money's worth. Students, it seems to me, are best as data collectors working under the close supervision of permanent senior staff members. If they come up with wonderfully bright ideas way beyond their job description and thus enhance you evaluation effort, all the better!

Clerical personnel can usually work less than full time or be shared because typical evaluations do not generate much typing between the period when proposals and research forms are being written and the final report. There are exceptions—such as evaluations that require transcriptions of tape recordings—but by and large the work is light. When workload is occasionally heavy, office temporaries can fill the need. Even if their rates are higher than regular people, it won't begin to approach the cost of continual clerical help.

A nice trick to save personnel costs is to borrow people for your work. You might request and receive a loan of personnel from a foundation or your local government or another agency with a particular interest in your evaluation. In the social service and criminal-justice areas, the interagency networks tend to be well developed and this is sometimes a real possibility. But of course someone has to have the nerve to ask, and negotiating may take a long time.

Joint evaluations with other agencies where costs are split was mentioned earlier and represents an outstanding route to cost savings. You might also be able to get valuable free help from an unpaid "advisory committee" whose personnel serve because they have competence in the area and a commitment to your organization.

DATA PROCESSING

The best way to cut costs in this area is simply not to use it. The purchase (for no more than $350) of a fancy office calculator may take care of your needs without any real computerizing of your data. Sometimes even a simple calculator and hand tabulating will do. If you've got a person on your staff already whose time is not expensive, this can be a perfectly satisfactory and cost-effective route.

If "computerizing" your data is unavoidable, as it is with studies having massive volumes of data, you will want to be sure you're doing it the most economical way. Best, of course, are services that are free. University computer centers sometimes provide nonprofit organizations with free programming help and processing time. You should definitely look into this kind of arrangement. A big advantage to these centers is that they usually maintain the kind of "packaged software" that is suitable for doing statistical tests on your data. If you had to purchase these same packages specifically for your use, your costs could be increased by thousands of dollars. I have had excellent experiences with university computer facilities, finding that they can satisfy all my data-analysis needs as long as I have one knowledgeable individual on my own staff. This person does not always have to be a programmer—just someone who is experienced in setting up data for computer analysis.

Of course if your agency already has its own computer, or shares one with other agencies, it would be nice to combine evaluation capacities with its data-storage and management-information ones. You may find that existing personnel will be able to suggest and implement low-cost data manipulations that are responsive to at least some of your evaluation questions. Or the addition of a programmer to handle research applications on your organization's computer may be less costly than farming out the work.

"Software houses" are the farms. Some are very good; they are used to handling research data and producing efficient reports. Others are nightmares to work with, do not meet deadlines, and are extremely expensive. It was my experience when I solicited bids from small software firms for analytic work that their bids varied by thousands of dollars on the same small job (between $2,500 and $4,800)! Try to find a reliable, objective adviser about these firms and avoid those with whom others have had trouble. A final note of caution is that firms always want extra money from you for services they claim you didn't specify at the beginning. Sometimes they're right, as when they have to clean up your data in some fashion, but it's something to think about when you're budgeting for data processing.

Keypunching is probably the most predictable data processing expense and one it's hard to pare down. The current rate in New York City is $.12–.25 for punching and verifying up to 80 card columns of data. I once tried optical scanning as an alternative to keypunching. I thought it would be cheaper because a local university was willing to donate time on an optical scanning machine. But the scanning sheets had to be prepared by hand, and personnel costs more than equaled keypunch savings.

MONEY, MONEY

Name a figure as high as you like in the hundreds of thousands of dollars. Believe it or not, there have been program evaluations that have cost that much. The really expensive ones tend to have federal funding, so it's actually we the taxpayers who have paid those incredible prices! Chances are you won't be in that kind of ballpark, which is generally limited to impact studies of national scope and importance. (Head Start springs immediately to mind.)

But even in less grandiose ballparks, you may also be interested in federal support. There are many federal agencies that provide funding for program evaluation. Notices of special funding competitions appear in the *Federal Register* publication (Note 19). (If your agency doesn't get it, major public libraries do.) This kind of support is very important for evaluation, especially as organizational budgets shrink and administrators are reluctant to spend dollars for evaluation that may have to be stolen from program work.

The biggest problem with special federal dollars is that they usually come with strings attached. The major string is that you have to do research that interests the funding agency. Even when there is general overlap with your interests, it may not be perfect and the emphasis may differ. They may be interested in theory, and you in practice. Or they may be interested in one aspect of your program, and you in the program as a whole. You may find yourself expending their resources to answer their questions and receive only marginal benefits in terms of your own. You can argue for (but cannot insist on) your own focus when you aren't paying the bills.

Special grants also require special applications. This may be a formidable process that requires your hiring an expert to assist you. Sometimes careful proposal writing can clarify your own thinking and better define your research questions. But other times it just seems to be a nuisance and to be planning "overkill." Funding agencies may also have elaborate reporting requirements once you've received the grant. I've already mentioned the requirement of an extensive "literature review" that I've had to live with, whether or not I felt the activity was useful or its breadth appropriate. There are formal progress reports to be produced and often a lengthy final report. The final report may take three months to write and may serve the funding agency's interests more than your own! Also, funders may retain for themselves the right to approve your staff, research forms, and techniques as you identify or develop them. They may insist that you hire outside research "experts" of a particular type. In sum, you should be sure that you need the federal dollars enough to make complying with their regulations worth the bargain.

Other levels of government may be able to assist you with evaluation funding, with less trouble for you. Look into what's available from state or regional public bodies. Sometimes it is not presented as dollars but rather contributions of personnel or services for evaluation work.

There is also supposed to be private foundation money around to fund evaluations. It has been my experience, however, that foundations are not particularly interested in funding program evaluation. They seem to prefer to fund the actual action programs, where they believe they will have more to show for their money. Also, compared with government grants, foundation assistance tends to be spread very thinly for any purpose.

A growing source of financial support for many community agencies is the private sector. Some large firms are becoming very socially conscious. (The reasons for it I will leave for your speculation.) Perhaps there is an organization in your area that would be interested in funding an evaluation of a tax-supported program as a way of demonstrating its sense of responsibility to the public. Good contacts are of particular use in selling and receiving this kind of support. As long as there is no conflict of interest involved and the organization is basically viewing it as a public service, you should not suffer from overmuch or inappropriate intrusion on your work.

Chapter 7

TALKING EVALUATIONESE

EVALUATIONESE ISN'T JARGONESE

You would never know it to read some evaluation reports, but American program evaluations can and should be run using the English language! If you're not insistent about this, you'll find someone talking about "non-schedule interviews employing informed premise questions where the group difference wasn't significant at the .05 level." That mouthful wouldn't bother many an academic researcher, and it (or a close cousin) might even crop up in an evaluation report being done for your organization if you don't guard against that possibility. Watch out for management consultants too; their jargon is different, but equally horrible!

You must insist that any outside experts or in-house research staff communicate with you in English. Almost anything they have to say can be put into nontechnical language without distorting its meaning. People who say this isn't true probably won't function very well outside their own technical world and would not be a good choice for your applied research work. In particular, evaluation reports should be written in readable fashion, perhaps with a glossary if any technical terms must be employed. You might want to build a requirement for lay-reader-type reports into an evaluation contract you enter: if you can't read it, you won't have to pay for it!

It's useful to learn some terms that succinctly express special evaluation concepts because this can help foster communication. But the line between useful special terms and jargon is insidiously slippery. There are many good research textbooks written for college students. Because evaluation basically *is* research, you could consult some of these books to gain a basic understanding of the key concepts that concern researchers (Note 20).

WHAT A FEW KEY TERMS MEAN

Samples.   Using a *sample* refers to choosing a limited number of cases (or people or places) to study in the hope that they will reflect the whole set of possible ones that could have been chosen (the *population*). It's time saving and money saving to limit the work in this way and sometimes it is the only feasible alternative when the population is very large.

Usually the aim of picking is to get a *representative* sample, one that represents the population it comes from. Talking with ten employees who you happen to know personally from among the 180 in your agency might give you an untrue picture of the state of employee morale. At some agencies (not yours, of course) your friends might tell you what they think you want to hear. You would do better to pick your informants in a random fashion. (You'd probably also get more candid information if you delegated the interviewing to someone they didn't feel they had to butter up.)

The size of a sample is also important. In the example of employee interviewing, ten out of 180 is undoubtedly too small. A general rule of thumb is that you need at least 30 units in a sample in order to draw reasonably confident conclusions from your findings. But if the population in which you're interested has 1800 individuals in it, you'd want to sample (yes, it can be used as a verb) more than 30 of them. Perhaps you have 1800 employees at three sites. You might want to talk with 30 at each site, and be able to learn something about site differences in morale as well as its overall level. If you were to choose 30 randomly from each site you'd have done a very sophisticated kind of thing called *stratified random sampling*. You picked randomly at each of several places (strata).

Samples can be chosen for different purposes too. They can be chosen to reflect certain characteristics, or they can be weighted in particular ways. There are experts in this field who hire out to the major U.S. polling companies and to the media. But your needs are likely to be far less fancy than TV networks trying to predict national election outcomes with a high degree of confidence from early polling returns.

Variables. Variables are, most basically, characteristics of people or things that you can measure. For example, height could be a variable in your evaluation work. You might want to measure the heights of children who had received food through a special nutrition program, and compare their heights with average figures for children of the same age and background. In this case height would be a *dependent* variable because it is conceptualized as depending on something else (in this case the program). Height is a *continuous* variable as well because there are no big gaps in the way it is measured. This is not true for a variable like gender, which has two possible values—male or female. This kind of variable is often referred to as a *nominal* or *categorical* variable because its values are measured by names or categories rather than by a set of numbers. *Ordinal* variables have a ranking order that goes beyond names, but isn't as precise as measuring something like height. When Clients answer a questionnaire saying they have benefited "moderately" from program service (as opposed to "tremendously" or "not at all"), they have provided data for the measurement of an ordinal variable, probably called something like "client satisfaction" by those who devised it.

The variable is the basic conceptual unit in almost all kinds of research, including evaluations. Client characteristics are really variables that can be measured; program characteristics are too; so are impacts. Are most clients *young* or *motivated*? Do they receive one *kind of service* or many? Do they get *better*? Many aspects of the operating environment are also likely to be conceived in this way. How *sympathetic* has top management been toward the program's goals? How has *health* in the city changed over time?

One of the toughest problems in any kind of research is translating the concept of the variable into something you will actually measure. For example, you may want to look at the amount of *recidivism* shown by a group of ex-offenders who went through a long therapy program. You could measure it by how many times they were rearrested and you might find, on average, a large number of rearrests. If you measured recidivism by convictions following criminal court appearances, you would probably see less "recidivism." But if you included those who had committed acts that violated the conditions under which they had been paroled from jail, the value of the variable would be way up again!

Statistical Significance.   When you measure variables, you often want to relate the measures to some standards or to compare them to each other. The discipline of statistics provides an array of tests to determine whether your measures depart "significantly" from what might be expected. A *statistically significant* finding is one that you can have confidence did not just arise by chance.

Statistically significant differences are not always *practically* important differences, however. When you are dealing with large samples, a difference can be "significant," but trivial in practical terms.

Control Groups.   The need for comparison data is very basic in research, and especially in evaluation research. You need to know whether your program is really responsible for certain outcomes or whether they would have occurred even in the absence of your program. A control group is an aggregation (usually of people) that does not get involved in the program you're studying at all. They are designated a special group (or groups) for comparison purposes only. If you've picked them randomly from among the same "pool" as those going into your program, then you'll have a true control group and can do an experimental evaluation. A typical evaluation experiment would involve the comparison of people going through a program with people who were eligible for the program but were randomly assigned to a control group instead. If the control group wasn't randomly assigned but rather consisted of individuals who hadn't met the program entrance requirements or who chose not to enter the program, then the basic element of a true experiment, random assignment, would not be present. *Random assignment* allows you to attribute outcome differences between those going through your program and those not going through it to effects from the program itself rather than to pre-existing differences between the groups.

WHY ALL THE FUSS ABOUT EXPERIMENTS?

Most social scientists will tell you that experiements are the best kind of research. And many funding agencies that are interested in definitive impact evaluations will insist on experimental design. Why do they care?

The basic reason is that an experimental design (where a true control group has been created) allows you to attribute later differences between the groups to the "treatment" that one of the groups of "subjects" has gotten. In evaluation research the *treatment* is the program you're evaluating.

If you used a less scientifically chosen comparison group, you might misattribute to your program a difference you measured later between the program group and the comparison people.

You will *not* want to run an experiment when your research questions relate to process more than impact. Nor will this kind of design be suitable for evaluating programs that are in flux. Experiments tend to take a long time, to be quite expensive, and to be difficult to operate in the real world outside of laboratory settings. For these reasons they are best where the evaluation is needed for major decision making—where you will decide whether to terminate or expand an important (and expensive) program. And of course you will want to employ this design where the time frame is leisurely enough to allow it. Decisions that must take place tomorrow won't be helped much by an evaluation design in which you'll still be picking subjects when tomorrow comes.

Other problems of running experiments are denying services to the control group and keeping subjects in their proper program and control groups long enough to follow them up. Denying services can sometimes present an ethical problem, but where a natural scarcity of the resource exists, this can be exploited. If your program can only take in half as many people as would be eligible, then you can decide who to take in by random assignment. Or, if people enter your program in phases, you can defer services for some through random assignment. These form *natural* experiments.

Keeping people in their respective groups can pose more of a problem. If your services are considered desirable, control-group designees have a way of popping up as participants in your program a short time later. And people in both groups have an unfortunate tendency to drop out and move away. Unfortunately you can't know whether those who departed were different from those who stayed—and in what ways. The cost factor of tracking your errant subjects can be prohibitive. And sometimes inducements have to be offered to get the cooperation of people in your control group who, unlike the treatment group, have no real reason for talking with you or agreeing to be observed or studied.

How would you get the cooperation of prostitutes who were designated to be part of a control group for a crime-control program? Paying the price of a "trick" to get a half-hour's interview with one of these ladies of the evening seemed unacceptably steep to me for some research I was designing!

Chapter 8

DESIGNING EVALUATION SO THAT YOU GET SOMETHING USEFUL OUT OF IT

LET YOUR EVALUATION QUESTIONS GUIDE YOU

Whether you are working with your own staff or with outside experts, it should be those questions of greatest concern to you and your organization that shape the research design. If you're primarily concerned with the status of project operations, you won't want to design an expensive impact study. And even if you're concerned about impact, you will probably also want to study program operations. Otherwise, you may be left with a "black box," meaning that you can't explain what happens between the inputs going into a program and its outcomes. Your questions may dictate a design that is sensitive to program side effects, or that taps attitudes of participants as well as "hard" data. You may care mainly about cost questions and be willing to sacrifice everything else.

A logical first step in the design process is to figure out *what kind of information* will be necessary and sufficient to answer your research questions. That is not to say you should guess what you'll find at the end of all your efforts, but rather you should be able to specify the general types of data you would need in order to draw meaningful conclusions from the evaluation. In my opinion, the most important thinking that's involved in research design is the kind you can do without much technical expertise. You need to think about what strategies are likely to give you the type of data you need to answer your questions—and answer them within the right scope, time frame, and budget. For example, to assess a rehabilitation program for the physically handicapped you might, at a minimum, want information about the clients' activities after receiving treatment. You could get this kind of information by asking them some simple questions over the telephone, which might be a perfectly adequate and low-budget approach to answering your questions. Or you might determine that you need more detailed information about activities and that it would be reasonable to get the information by asking a number of clients to keep a daily log of where they have been each day. If *changes* in activity as a result of the treatment are of greater interest to you than just *amounts* of activity, then you will also want the patients to keep pretreatment logs for comparison purposes. Since it could be a substantial research effort to follow up all these logs, you would have to decide whether you want the information enough to expend the necessary resources.

If you are concerned about whether your new office arrangements reduce difficulty for clients dealing with your agency, you will surely want to collect some information about how complex things are these days. Would checking clients' completeness in filling out your new forms as opposed to your old forms be sufficient for your purpose? Perhaps, and you could collect this data fairly easily by going through a sample of forms from before and after the innovation. Or you may feel that you need more information about any remaining sources of difficulty to properly evaluate your innovation and address your concern. To do this, you might want and need to design a study that included interviewing of clients, and perhaps systematic observation of office procedures. But in this case, more time and expense will be involved.

What if you've got lots of questions about the impact of a

community health-education program you're running. You want information about changes in local hospital clinic use, changes in people's health status, in immunization completeness, and in attitudes toward health care. Wow, that's a tall order! You may be able to get access to summary hospital statistics to answer your question about changes in clinic use. And you might be able to come up with imaginative, fairly inexpensive kinds of data collection to tackle your questions about changes in community-health status and immunizations. For example, you could look at public-health data on the incidence of certain diseases like VD to see if your neighborhood has shown a different pattern of incidence from other neighborhoods. And perhaps the local schools would provide summary data on the immunization completeness of neighborhood children being registered for kindergarten. These kinds of data-collection methods can almost certainly take place within your budget and time frame.

Data to answer attitudinal questions may be more costly to collect. You will need responses from a substantial sample of people who have been served by your program. You may be able to catch some people to interview right at the program. A telephone survey is also a possibility. Personal visits to conduct interviews cost more than many evaluations will be able to budget! (You will want responses from those who haven't been served, as well, if your questions require comparisons.)

TAKE OUT INSURANCE ON USEFULNESS

I couldn't begin to tell you how many dollars have been poured into program evaluations that yielded no practically useful information. While you can't get a guarantee that any research will have a fabulous "payoff," intelligent designing at the beginning improves your chances. Try to build in techniques that will produce useful information for you regardless of whether the data "come out" one way or another.

In general, utility will be enhanced if you avoid the kind of black-box research referred to earlier, if you collect data of more than one sort to address the same set of questions, and if you use proven methods. A study that looks at how your program operates as well as the outcomes it produces should provide very useful information about why it achieved whatever results it did—either benefits or disappointments. Repeated evaluations of treatment programs for criminal-justice clients have come up with findings of very little effect on recidivism (Note 21). New evaluations that look only at recidivism are unlikely to produce valuable findings.

And collecting data from different sources improves the likelihood that you will have useful findings. If one of the methods doesn't work, you will be able to fall back on something else. And if one method yields data that are only slightly suggestive of something, you will have data generated by another method to either corroborate or refute the suggestion. In general, choosing at least one method that has been successfully used for a similar purpose in the past is good insurance against things failing to work out completely.

FORCE YOURSELF TO LOOK AHEAD

In keeping with those little signs that humorously exhort you to plan ahead, it's important to try to wind up with sufficient and appropriate data to answer your questions. You don't want to use such a small sample that people scoff at your conclusions. Nor do you want to have lots of data, but none to provide clues as to *why* a program is having an effect (or isn't). You may need examples of actual program events for your final report.

But you also want to avoid gathering too much data, so that there is no time or staff for its analysis. Your organization's posterity is unlikely to appreciate file cabinets crammed full of unanalyzed out-of-date data that you gathered because "someone might want it some day"!

While you won't be able to predict what your actual findings will be (unless you're really cheating!), you should be able to lay out most of the tables of data you will want in your final report before you even begin the research. Basically the tables will summarize relationships between and among program, client, and context variables. With a little intellectual exercise, you can translate your research questions into the kinds of data you will want and then into the categories in which you will want them. If you care about whether younger children show slower progress in art therapy, you will want to examine a table of data arranging progress of art-therapy clients according to their ages. Or you might need a table that breaks down the age-progress relationship for three different types of art therapy that your program employs. And, in fact, if you develop some skill at this aspect of design work, you may be able to teach it to your experts. It's a real knack to be able to force yourself to look ahead, anticipate what you'll need, and make sure the specific research that gets designed will allow you to get it and present it to your organization.

You can embark on an evaluation with design plans ranging from the short-term to the remote future, but you're probably better off if your thinking is relatively short range. The goals of many organizations have a way of changing over the long haul, and so do the personnel involved with them! You can plan evaluation as a staged process, to proceed only if the prior step has resulted in something of value to your agency (or laid a solid groundwork for something of value). Or you could use an initial phase of research to make program modifications and contemplate further evaluation—really a cycle concept. This is similar to the *action research* model employed by some social scientists. A concept is tried out in an action program, the program process is studied, and the program is tinkered with according to the implications of the research findings. It can be particularly useful when a basic concept has demonstrated its value and you're interested in fine tuning; or, in exactly the opposite situation, it can help you clarify initially vague plans about how your program should be shaped.

Chapter 9

LIKE, FOR INSTANCE . . .

BEFORE-AND-AFTER STUDIES

You can evaluate a new program by looking for changes that it appears to create. These might be changes in the condition or skills of the group served by the program or changes in the system within which the program operates. You'll need preprogram measures for this kind of evaluation design, but sometimes you can collect them retrospectively after the program has begun. Generally, researchers view this kind of design as weak when measures have been taken at only two points in time, as with test scores or blood-sugar levels. You won't know whether the differences were greater than those that would have occurred in the course of normal fluctuations. Taking measures at a number of points will give you time-series data, and this has become very popular among research people. A series of measures is often available from files and existing records perhaps already on your information system. A series allows you to see whether pre/postprogram differences are greater than differences that show up in the normal course of taking repeated measures either before or after a program has begun.

COMPARISON-GROUP STUDIES

This is probably the most common evaluation design. People who will not participate in the program, but look similar to the program group in other ways, are designated to be a comparison group. You assume that any differences between the groups that you find later are due to the effects of the program. Sometimes you will be in error, because the groups weren't really all that similar in some way. For example, last year's first-grade classes may have been brighter than this year's, or people diagnosed as schizophrenic in Cleveland may be only neurotic in New York. But a comparison-group study is an economical design and is often the only choice for an evaluator. You can have more than one comparison group too, which can give you additional information and sometimes add to the confidence you place in your findings. It is not unusual to draw comparison groups from several geographical sites where people may be receiving different kinds of programs rather than none at all. Then the various sites can actually constitute comparison groups for each other!

Assuming you can get cooperation from your comparison group(s), only ingenuity, time, and money need limit the kinds of data you collect on both groups. You can use existing records, do interviews, supply questionnaires, make observations, or do all of these! (You may be limited to existing records if your comparison group isn't interested in being studied and can't be paid off.)

EXPERIMENTS

As you've already read, this kind of design is the academic researcher's dream. Using a randomly selected control group or groups means that you can more confidently attribute later group differences to your program. You may find it easy to create a control group when you're running a popular program. If fewer people can be handled than those who apply, participation can be determined by lottery. Those who are chosen for the control group might even be offered the service at a later data, to assuage ethical concerns and to gain better cooperation from these people. But remember, if you're thinking of a major experiment, that experiments tend to be lengthy and difficult to hold together. Your evaluation questions should be equally major—questions about long-term program impacts on people's lives or possible expansions of highly costly program models.

DETAILED CASE STUDIES

It will sometimes be appropriate to evaluate programs by focusing on the experiences of a few participants. If the program is brand new or your evaluation questions relate mainly to program process and operation, you may learn a great deal from the case-study approach. You would probably do extensive interviewing of selected participants and staff, and might choose to make tape recordings, films, or first-hand observations of project events. Any reports should be careful to conceal personal identities. Findings are likely to be more suggestive than definitive, but can point to particular program problems and successes, as well as possible modifications.

You can also use case studies to supplement and enliven more formal evaluation designs. Remember that you don't want to find yourself with outcome measures but no idea what produced them.

ANALYSIS OF PROGRAM COSTS

On their own, or in combination with other approaches, cost analysis techniques are important tools.

Simple cost analysis involves accounting for all budgeted or actual project expenditures, even when they do not appear in the project's budget. Experts would be able to tell you about "hidden costs" and other tricky matters—economies of scale, indirect costs, etc. You can compare the cost of your program with others that are similar or you can look at your program's cost factors as a separate issue.

More elegant cost analyses take project outcomes into account. Cost-effectiveness analysis can tell you what it costs to serve one client for one day or process one case to completion or improve scholastic level one year. You can compare unit costs of your program to other programs or to standard operating procedures. Economists tend to feed easily available data into cost-effectiveness analyses, so you shouldn't allow this kind of expert to go his or her way unchallenged. You may have to choose between using existing outcome data whose reliability you question and doing expensive original data collection. The results of your analysis—no matter how impressive all the numbers and dollar signs appear—will be only as dependable as the data that were used.

Cost-benefit analysis is an extension of cost-effectiveness techniques to place dollar prices on outcomes. Where this is feasible, you can obtain very useful ratios of program benefits to costs. But again, bear in mind that your findings rest entirely on the data that was input; if the data were inaccurate or based on erroneous assumptions, ratios won't be useful for much beyond impressing yourself or your organization. And it's very hard to place dollar values on outcomes of social programs that are usually measured only in humanistic terms.

OTHER APPROACHES

For practical needs, you are probably best off with simple, traditional evaluation designs. But your organization may have unique programs and responsibilities that are best assessed in special ways.

Computer simulations can be used to look at certain kinds of problems and alternative strategies for their solution. You will almost certainly need some expert help with this kind of evaluation work, but in return you might discover ways to improve your operations. I know of simulations that exist to aid the assignment of police-patrol personnel, and at least some people think they are quite useful (Riccio, Note 22).

Other innovative approaches are possible, but beware of gimmicks cloaked in jargon. As I keep reassuring you, your good sense will be your most valuable evaluation design aid.

Chapter 10

LIVING THROUGH AN EVALUATION

GETTING TO THE NITTY-GRITTY

Once you've gotten through the planning stage (or become sufficiently impatient with it) you'll want to get on with some "doing." But the beginnings of action in an evaluation may not seem all that different from planning, and it's really not a sharp transition. You (or your experts) will be thinking about the methods you'll use and then you'll actually pilot using them. You might be writing, trying out and polishing up the wording of a survey. You could be testing the feasibility of interviewing people over the phone as opposed to in person. You may be establishing an early "presence" at a site you will be observing intensively.

I once worked with a valued research associate on a study of police. We were testing out some forms for recording observations of how the police went about their business. You can imagine the surprise of one policeman who was told by my very physically attractive female colleague that she was "refining our instruments" and would he please help her out?! After our blushes faded, we went back to the task at hand because pilot testing is extremely important in all evaluation work. It's really reality testing to see if what you've planned is likely to work the way you thought it would. Perhaps you hadn't realized how infrequently certain events can be seen, or that people are not as eager as you thought they would be to tell you about their methods of contraception. You may need to do a lot of revising to bring your evaluation work down to earth.

Lost in the Fields

Moving into active data collection is likely to mean a physical move too —from planning, which was based in your office, to data collecting at the program sites or elsewhere in the outside world. Researchers like to call all these non-office locales "the field," and have a tendency to be very vague about their precise whereabouts in these fields. It's my impression that this occupational quirk also pops up among caseworkers of varying sorts and traveling salespeople.

What researchers do while in the field must cover a multitude of sins, but it's up to those supervising the research to also get out into the field to make sure that data collecting is done as planned. This is particularly important if you use an outside consulting firm.

Maintaining Control

Especially if you're involved in a study of some size, the "fieldwork" tends to go on and on. It's important for somebody at your agency to be on top of things—to be evaluating both the evaluation and the evaluators. You need to make sure that deadlines are being met. If you didn't already build them into a contract, then establishing interim deadlines for parts of the data collection to be completed is a good idea.

You should insist on documentation on all aspects of the research effort. While you might get accused of being too much of a bureaucrat, I suggest you persist because being a patsy seems to me to be far worse. Without adequate written explanations of what has been done and not done (and the reasons), you may be left with nothing if your evaluators don't see the job through. This applies to both in-house and outside experts. It's terribly hard to pick up a study from someone who had it all in his or her head!

Lots of documenting in the form of memos and interim reports also can be an invaluable help to writing a final research report some time later. And since at least some part of this task often falls to an administrator, you may be the beneficiary! And if you actually read the research memos and talk with others at your agency about them, at least you might acquire a reputation for being something of a research expert yourself (although it is hoped you will never have to deliver more than you're capable of)!

CHANGES

Changes—in the research questions you care about or in the program over time—are a challenge to research. You could begin by questioning "Does our program rehabilitate alcoholics?" and, with increasing cynicism about the likelihood of rehabilitation, decide that in fairness you can only ask "Does our project provide humane treatment to alcoholics?"

Flexibility is generally a very desirable quality to cultivate in seeing evaluation work through to a conclusion. If your research questions change (for example, because your agency has a new director or a new mandate) you will want to be able to change your research accordingly. The suggestion made in the last chapter about phased research implementation lends itself well to this kind of flexibility. Long-term contracts with federal funding sources are more likely to lock you into your designs and reduce your flexibility. But there may still be room for constructive maneuvering if you recognize that your design is outdated or inappropriate.

You should occasionally refer back to the research questions that were your starting point. If they're still current, great! If they're not, they should be changed. In either case, you should periodically reassess whether the work that's going on will be able to provide answers to the research questions that are current.

Program changes pose a different kind of challenge. They may be entirely out of your control. I was once involved in an evaluation that was planned as an elaborate study that would track waves of police-academy graduates over time. But before that study could get off the ground, a budget crisis cancelled the hiring of the waves that were to be studied. Some imaginative redesigning was required to develop a meaningful study with a much smaller target group.

Sometimes unexpected but nice things happen to you in the course of conducting your research. An oppportunity to collect a unique kind of data may arise, or you might realize that something you're doing could be done a lot more simply than you planned. You should take advantage of such serendipitous developments. It may mean a bit of juggling of your plans and resources, but being flexible might result in very interesting findings. An organization that was the subject of a study I did asked for data on a particular program question. We changed our research design to respond to their request, found some fairly interesting things, and generated lots of good will.

But if you become convinced that you are getting much less than you expected from the expense and effort involved in your evaluation, you should consider cutting it short. Within the limits of your contractual arrangements (and your lawyers should have built in broad limits), you should exercise your cancelling option when you are extremely dissatisfied. What are the problems that can arise? Well, I'm always being surprised with new possibilities, but I'll discuss a few below, by way of example.

TROUBLESHOOTING

Research vs. Operations. A very common kind of problem interfering with smooth data collection is conflict between research needs and program operations. The problems can take different forms. Sometimes research staff actually interfere with operations; other times it is more perception than fact. When program staff have been asked to act as data collectors for the research, this can potentially create conflicts that interfere with both research and operations. Often the problems can be worked out by a sensitive administrator who is prepared to listen to all the points of view involved. (Is this you?) You may have to run interference for research people with program operators, or convince research people to leave their tape recorders back at the office. You may need to limit research access —or to expand it. You may have to "take a side." Basically this kind of problem draws on the same management skills you bring to other organizational headaches.

The Law and Research.   Other common problems encountered by evaluators are legal ones. One very important aspect of research work that is governed by both federal and state statutes is confidentiality of research data. If you intend to collect data that identify specific private persons (either by name or by unique characteristics), you should do some preparatory legal research to be sure that problems aren't going to crop up later. You may be required to do any one of a number of things to "protect the privacy" of the individuals you are studying. When you receive government funding for your evaluation work, their requirements in this area will usually be made explicit to you. You may have to sign an assurance about certain procedures and data storage arrangements.

The most troublesome requirements that regulations or statutes may require of you is "informed consent," that is, telling people what the research is about and letting them decide whether to participate. Sometimes you must get their agreement in writing. My advice, if you are faced with a situation like this, is to reconsider whether you really need to collect data on individuals. Remember that privacy regulations and statutes only apply to that kind of data, not to collecting data that is anonymous or has already been added up for sets of individuals ("aggregated").

Other legal problems occasionally arise, but they are rare. If you plan to station observers in dangerous settings, this is a legal concern because someone has to assume responsibility. If you send out interviewers to make home visits in high-crime neighborhoods, you may have to think about liability there too. (It may be prudent to send them out in pairs.)

˜ *Falsification of Data and Other Nightmares.*   At least a bit of fraud exists in every field. It's not my impression that research has more than its share, but even a little bit should be too much for you. You'll certainly want to do enough spot-checking and auditing of evaluation data and fieldwork to assure yourself that your findings will be honest. Finding out later that some parts of your data are fraudulent is truly a nightmare, but I have known researchers who had to salvage a very major study under those conditions.

Paying interviewers by the hour rather than by the interview is helpful for preventing slipshod work and downright invention. And getting interim reports of research findings will at least suggest that a steady stream of information is being assembled and analyzed; marathon now-or-never write-ups at the ends of projects encourage fictionalizing when it is realized that not all the needed data was collected.

Delays, Delays, Delays.   Perhaps because there are so many stages through which an evaluation must progress, there are bound to be delays. You should expect some, as you would with your normal administrative operations.

If things are slow to get started, you may want to extend the timetable for the research (providing that your timetable for decision making will allow it). Delays in collecting or analyzing data may be trivial or serious. Sometimes they arise from lack of adequate planning or pilot testing. Sometimes they are unavoidable snags that are best taken with a bit of humor.

If you find that deadlines are seriously overdue, however, you will certainly want to exercise whatever control you possess in the situation. This could extend to cancelling the remainder of a study or, if it is too late for that, shaming or threatening the procrastinators. I found myself in one unfortunate situation of this sort where an important portion of an evaluation write-up was long overdue from an ex-employee. My big error was to have ever acceded to the fellow becoming an ex-employee when the final work product had not yet been delivered. There were very few sanctions I could use later.

Chapter 11

"WHAT ARE ALL THOSE
GREEK SYMBOLS?"

Data analyses range from the direct and simple to the extremely elaborate. Chances are you'll want something simple to satisfy the practical evaluation questions you framed. But even then, you will certainly want to use some statistics; even a percentage is a statistic! And you will undoubtedly want to report percentages and averages, two of the most common kinds of descriptive statistics.

Whether you need to go further will depend on your data. If you have come up with dramatic numbers, the results will probably speak for themselves. If a measure of change or group difference is impressively high (or low), your findings will receive attention and have practical importance to your audience. You won't be very concerned with applying tests to see if that difference measures up in some technical sense. But these kinds of tests can tell you how likely it is that your result is real, and not a fluke that occurred by chance. And when your numbers are not too dramatic, this can be useful information to have.

The simplest tests can be intuitively understood even if their Greek symbols remain somewhat mysterious. The famous "t-test" tells you how likely it is that an average arithmetic value or percentage that you found in your sample of cases truly differs from some other value (for example, zero or another group's average or percentage). The usual standard for "truth" is whether there is no more than a one percent (or five percent) probability that you've got a fluke result. For example, you could look at whether a three percent increase in illness recovery rate under your new program would be expected from chance fluctuations anyway.

Another relatively simple and common test is the "Chi-square" test. It allows you to test differences among numbers of people, places, or things that you have tabulated. This test is also an aid to interpreting whether differences that emerge are "true" and not likely to have arisen just by chance. For example, you could see whether your program is taking in disproportionately more women since it started a special outreach to women's groups.

Statistical tests exist that look at trends, measure the degree of association between two variables, break down the relative effects of many variables on some outcome, and do a huge number of other things. They are often accompanied by fancy Greek-symbol notation and can be understood by only a tiny fraction of the national population. Unless your funding source *requires* a sophisticated type of analysis, you will probably do best with simple statistical methods even if they are not as precise or definitive as fancier tests. Otherwise, while your report may speak eloquently to academic people, it's going to leave you and your agency's decision makers at the fringe of understanding. You may be left to interpret complex statistical inferences to those who know less than yourself.

You are likely to confront the concept of *statistical significance* even if you don't venture into anything fancy. The concept of statistical significance, also discussed in Chapter 7, refers to numerical outcomes that are unlikely to have arisen by chance, and which are likely to represent "true" values that would emerge if you measured every possible case that you could have measured. Differences that look dramatic are likely also to be statistically significant. But the converse isn't necessarily true. Many statistically significant differences are trivial in practical terms, and good only for upholding preconceived points of view in evaluation reports. So I suggest that you bring your common sense to bear in this area. Even if a statistically significant two percent increase is observed in the number of dental checkups kids in a program target neighborhood receive, you've got to decide whether this two percent difference has any practical importance. There are differences that just don't make any difference!

COMPUTER ANALYSES

It is indisputable that computers have made research with large samples manageable. The kind of survey that used to require a year of data analysis by hand usually didn't get done. If your research questions require you to have a very large sample or data base, you will probably want to handle your data by machine analysis.

If you are taking the computer route, you will almost certainly have to rely on some "experts." These experts, like others, should be judged primarily on their past performance and on their ability to speak your language and be concerned with your concerns. You won't want a brilliant programmer who lives in his own world, or a software firm that has never gotten a job done on time in its life! Remember that costs vary widely. Make sure to get several competitive bids if you're going outside your organization for help. If you have someone write a simple computer program for you, then the analysis can be done at a convenient computer installation (your own organization's, if you have it). The format of the printouts can be tailored to your needs. There are also several ready-made "packages" of computer programs for statistical analyses. These packages are found mainly at university computer facilities. They are quite versatile, going way beyond what you're likely to need for evaluation research. Some can even spew out graphs with plots of your data. They may also prove economical, because you can save programming costs.

Do you Really Need a Computer?

For all but very large sample studies, you will probably *not* need or benefit from computer analysis of your data. Using a computer can be expensive "overkill," which will delay your progress, give you headaches, and not substantially improve what ·you've learned. Data has to be prepared for a machine and that can be time consuming and costly; programs have to be found, written, or purchased; and "bugs" have to be ironed out.

In general, the new electronic calculators that you or your staff can operate from the hand or desk top are likely to meet your data-analysis needs. Manual tabulating may still need to be done, but a very great advantage of processing your data without a computer is the closeness you will have to it. You can *feel* the quality of the data—whether it's tight or sloppy, complete or not. You can spot errors with relative ease. Computers may move decimal points with impunity, drop half of your cases from the analysis, or give you gibberish for "output"—and the worst thing is that you may never notice it! When you're handling the data yourself, you're not distanced from it in this way.

But, it must be admitted, there are analyses that are feasible only on a machine (such as multiple regression) and there are data bases so large that you could drown in efforts to push them around by hand. But make sure during the design stage that you really want a study so large that you must use a computer for data analysis.

What does It All Mean?

There are plenty of researchers around who can churn out data analyses and write voluminous reports of their findings, but who give very little thought to what they've really come up with. You must make sure that this doesn't happen to you and your organization. Make sure that those doing the data analysis are forced to go beyond a summary of the statistics they've produced. They should structure those statistics to provide their best interpretation of what the figures mean. They should look at the results in terms of your original questions. For example, if your study of group homes was conducted to find out how many staff were enough, you'll certainly want this question addressed! They should show you trends in the data using graphs; they should provide tabular comparisons of groups or sites, where it would make a point. They should "disaggregate" overall numbers that mask important components.

There is a high degree of skill involved in interpreting numbers—and in designing charts and graphs that express what's present in the findings. You should certainly involve yourself in the process of interpretation because you know your agency well and can make judgments about practical implications—for example, how important is a particular amount of improvement. But don't let the analysts turn over uninterpreted statistics to you, saying you can make best sense of them. It is often a huge and complex job, and that's one of the reasons you wanted an analyst in the first place.

We're all vulnerable to our biases in interpreting statistics so that if you're interested in getting honest answers to your questions, the more objectivity that can be brought to bear on interpreting findings, the better. There's a delightful book from the 1950s called *How to Lie With Statistics* by Darrel Huff (Note 23). What Huff really talks about is how people report statistical findings so that they present a point of view. For example, you may want to graph venereal disease decline since the start of your v.d. publicity program. A decline of 80 cases will look far more dramatic if you draw a vertical axis that only goes up to 100 cases rather than 500. What you finally say your data mean must, of course, be a matter between you and your conscience.

Chapter 12

THE END—IT DOESN'T HAVE
TO BE BITTER

PREVIEWS OF THE FINAL REPORT

When your findings and tentative interpretations are ready, you will certainly want to share them with others in leadership at your organization. Especially if findings are dramatic or controversial, you will want others to preview them before the evaluation report gets beyond draft form. Without such previews, you may find yourself issuing a report from out on some limb. Early internal debate over the meaning of the results is appropriate at this early stage, and you may even find the process helpful to your own thinking. What seems to you to be a program operating according to design may look to others examining the data like several harried caseworkers who are spread too thinly. Someone may see a favorable program impact depending solely on a selective intake policy. Others may argue that discernible system improvement is more meaningful than negative findings on client improvement.

When the findings are weak in policy implications (or just plain wishy-washy), a previewing process will not be nearly as interesting, and in fact only the evaluators and yourself are likely to care very much about the study at that point. Unfortunately there's not very much you can do about disappointing findings. Occasionally you will have framed good research questions, designed a study to produce useful information, conducted the study conscientiously, and come up with nothing exciting. It happens.

In any case, a bit of stock taking is helpful before you start writing your final report. You should be sure that data analysis and interpretation have been reasonably thorough and that you have something to say in a report. Try to outline what you think the important findings were. See if anyone agrees with you!

THE FINAL DOCUMENT

Getting out a report on an evaluation can be very straightforward. Particularly if your study was simple and intended solely for an in-house audience, you can write a brief document—no more than 20 pages—explaining your guiding questions, what you did, what you found, and any recommendations that stem from the research. You will probably want to make charts or graphs to point up noteworthy findings.

If you are doing the research with outside financial support or if the audience for your report will be wider than your own "shop," you will need a more elaborate product. You will probably want a general statement of the problems you were addressing and some background on them. Your description of the methods used will require some detail. The findings will probably be presented in a set of tables and figures. Conclusions will need to be stated fairly broadly, so that they are of interest to people outside your agency as well as in it. Try not to have the major conclusion be that more research is needed. (It's like a slap in the face to those who spent money on what you already did. And it looks like the evaluators just want to feather their nests!) You may want to consider writing an *executive summary* of several pages—a briefer version of the long report and somewhat similar to what you'd prepare for a small study. If you write an executive summary, give it your best effort so that condensing your points doesn't distort them. Most people, given the choice, will read only the summary.

If you're preparing a report for wide distribution, you'll want to be sure that you've given credit where it's due. Evaluators like to have their names on their reports as authors, and generally your organization should try to accommodate. A mention in an "acknowledgements" section is nice, but the major contributors should be named as authors.

Getting some editing help is likely to make a more readable final product. But take care that editors don't delay the report until it is no longer timely. I was once asked to wait for a brief legal review of one of my reports; though I ended up with beautifully edited prose, it was six months later! Editing can also result in changes of emphasis and this is something you will want to watch carefully so that the final report still concludes what you concluded.

SPREADING IT AROUND

The extent to which you'll distribute an evaluation report will depend on why the study got started. If it was to inform decision makers about particular questions, then they should be the major recipients of the finished report. Your report may be only one factor in the decision process but if it's well done and ready on time, you can certainly expect it to receive serious attention. If your study was intended to inform a state legislature or commission, you may want very wide distribution. Especially if your guiding questions are of general interest and your findings clearcut, you may want to circulate your report to the media and otherwise publicize it. If you try to use the media, especially newspapers, I must caution you that their excerpting of research reports can produce stories that are inaccurate or misleading. It has been my experience to have an extremely reputable paper write the results of one of my studies accurately, but to have some editor put a totally contradictory subhead in bold type above one of the paragraphs. Writing your own news releases, as your agency may already do about nonresearch events, seems to produce the most accurate reporting. If you began with a bias—a hidden or not-so-hidden agenda, and your expectations were confirmed, you or others may want to use the study for advocacy purposes. Copies of evaluations are often sent to places where it is felt they will influence opinions.

Personal briefings and presentations of evaluation findings are an excellent way of getting the word around. As I mentioned earlier, it is smart to offer prereport briefings to management in your agency, but other employees will also want to hear what you've found. And groups from outside your agency may be interested audiences as well. You may even find unanticipated attention to your work—other jurisdictions or people having a different perspective on your topic area. You may have done a study of comparative elementary school curricula that is of considerable interest to organized women's groups or to the U.N.!

But you should be aware that evaluation reports, no matter how dramatic the results, do not automatically influence policy decisions. If you want a report you've worked on to be heeded, the burden is yours to push it. Experts in evaluation have been notoriously poor at this. And while some of their professional organizations are trying to get them to do better, don't wait! If worthwhile information is available from what you've done, you'll have to reach out to interest and educate decision makers. Perhaps you can convince them, as I hope I've convinced you, that program evaluation can be a useful, down-to-earth tool for practical people.

NOTES

1. New York State Division of Criminal Justice Services developed and implemented a performance evaluation system from 1977 to 1979.
2. The United States Department of Health, Education and Welfare transferred Medicare payments to EASYRIDE paratransit service operated by the Vera Institute of Justice, New York City, 1976 to 1980.
3. Rosenthal, Robert. *Experimenter effects in behavioral research*. New York: Appleton-Century-Crofts, 1966. See also: Rosenthal, R., & Jacobson, L. *Pygmalion in the classroom: Teacher expectation and pupils' intellectual development*. New York: Holt, Rinehart and Winston, 1968.
4. Sichel, J. L., Friedman, L. N., Quint, J. C., & Smith, M. E. *Final report: Women on patrol*. Washington, D.C.: National Institute of Law Enforcement and Criminal Justice, January 1978.
5. Kinsey, A. C., Pomeroy, W. B., & Martin, C. E. *Sexual behavior in the human male*. Philadelphia: W. B. Saunders, 1948.
6. For example: Department of Health, Education and Welfare—Code of Federal Regulation (45 CFR 46); Department of Justice, Law Enforcement Assistance Administration—Confidentiality of Identifiable Research and Statistical Information.
7. Ross, H. Laurence, Campbell, Donald T., & Glass, Gene V. Determining the social effects of a legal reform. *American Behavioral Scientist,* 1970, *13,* 493–509.

8. Campbell, D. T., & Ross, L. The Connecticut crackdown on speeding: Time-series data in quasi-experimental analysis. *Law and Society Review,* 1968, *3,* 33–53.
9. *The nation's toughest drug law: Evaluating the New York experience.* Washington, D.C.: National Institute of Law Enforcement and Criminal Justice, March 1978.
10. PROMIS research project, Institute for Law and Social Research, Washington, D.C.
11. For example, see: Kerlinger, Fred N., & Pedhazur, Elazar J. *Multiple regression in behavioral research.* New York: Holt, Rinehart and Winston, 1973. Also see: Cohen, Jacob, & Cohen, Patricia. *Applied multiple regression/correlation analysis for the behavioral sciences.* New York: John Wiley, 1975.
12. Greenwald, Judith E., & Connolly, Harriet A. *Policewomen on patrol: New York City.* Unpublished manuscript, City University of New York/Urban Institute, Washington, D.C., 1974.
13. Fishman, Robert. *An evaluation of criminal recidivism in projects providing rehabilitation and diversion services in New York City,* Criminal Justice Coordinating Council, New York City, 1975.
14. For example, the Inter-University Consortium for Political and Social Science Research at the University of Michigan maintains extensive data archives, listed in *Guide to Resources and Services,* 1980–1981.
15. City University of New York—New York City Police Department, planning seminars for neighborhood police teams experiment, autumn 1971.
16. Bronx Coordinated Anti-Arson Project, New York City, 1978.
17. Priority prosecution study, Criminal Justice Coordinating Council, New York City, funded by New York State Division of Criminal Justice Services, 1977–1979.
18. Vera Institute of Justice, New York City.
19. *Federal Register* is published daily by the U.S. Government Printing Office, Washington, D.C.
20. For example: Selltiz, Claire, et al. *Research methods in social relations.* New York: Holt, Rinehart and Winston, 1959.
21. Lipton, D., Martinson, R., & Wilks, J. *The effectiveness of correctional treatment: A survey of treatment evaluation studies.* New York: Praeger, 1975. Also: Bailey, Walter C. Correctional outcome: An evaluation of 100 reports. In *Crime and Justice.* New York: Basic Books, 1971.
22. Riccio, Lucius J. Direct deterrence: An analysis of the effectiveness of police patrol and other crime prevention technologies. *Journal of Criminal Justice,* 1974, *2,* 207–217.
23. Huff, Darrell. *How to lie with statistics.* New York: W. W. Norton, 1954.

IF YOU WANT TO DO
FURTHER READING

The articles and books listed in this bibliography are recommended to the planner or administrator who wishes to learn more about program evaluation. While few of the references read like novels, none are highly technical. Many have a practical emphasis, as their titles suggest. Almost all of the references can be found in a university library or can be ordered by mail from the publisher. Hard-to-find items have, for the most part, been excluded.

While a smattering of articles report on particular evaluation studies and some articles and books pertain to a particular field, most are of general interest. Perhaps one or two will interest you enough to seek them out.

Abt, Clark C. The state of the art of program evaluation. *Legislative oversight and program evaluation*. Washington, D.C.: U.S. Government Printing Office, May 1976.

Abt, Clark C., ed. *The evaluation of social programs*. Beverly Hills: Sage Publications, 1976.

Abt, Clark C. The public good, the private good, and the government good in the evaluation of social programs: How inept government requirements increase costs and reduce effectiveness. *Evaluation Quarterly,* November 1978, *2,* 620–630.

Agency for International Development. *Evaluation handbook.* Washington, D.C.: U.S. Government Printing Office, 1971.

American Institutes for Research. *Evaluative research strategies and methods.* Pittsburgh, Pa., 1970.

Anderson, Scarvia B., & Ball, Samuel. *The profession and practice of program evaluation.* San Francisco: Jossey-Bass, 1978.

Andrew, Gwen. Some observations on management problems in applied social research. *The American Sociologist,* 1967, *2,* 84–89.

Angrist, S. S. Evaluation research: Possibilities and limitations. *Journal of Applied Behavioral Science,* 1975, *11,* 75–91.

Aronson, Sidney H., & Sherwood, Clarence C. Researcher versus practitioner: Problems in social action research. *Social Work,* 1967, *12,* 89–96.

Babbie, E. R. *Survey research methods.* Belmont, Calif.: Wadsworth, 1973.

Banner, David K., et al. *The politics of social program evaluation.* Cambridge, Mass.: Ballinger Publishing Co., 1975.

Bateman, Worth. Assessing program effectiveness: A rating system for identifying relative program success. *Welfare in Review,* 1968, *6,* 1–10.

Beckman, Norman. Congressional Research Service: Resources for oversight and evaluation. *Legislative oversight and program evaluation.* Washington, D.C.: U.S. Government Printing Office, May 1976.

Berk, Richard A., & Rossi, Peter H. Doing good or worse: Evaluation research politically reexamined. *Social Problems,* 1976, *23,* 337–349. Also in *Evaluation studies review annual,* Vol. 2. Marcia Guttentag, ed. Beverly Hills, Calif.: Sage Publications, 1977.

Berlak, Harold. Values, goals, public policy and educational evaluation. *Review of Educational Research,* 1970, *40,* 261–278.

Berry, Dean. *The politics of personnel research.* Ann Arbor, Mich.: University of Michigan, 1967.

Biderman, Albert D., & Sharp, Laure M. *The competitive evaluation research industry.* Washington, D.C.: Bureau of Social Science Research, 1972.

Biderman, Albert D., & Sharp, Laure M. The evaluation research community: RFP readers, bidders, and winners. *Evaluation,* 1974, *2,* 36–40.

Bigman, Stanley K. Evaluating the effectiveness of religious programs. *Review of Religious Research.* 1961, *2,* 97–121.

Binner, P. R. Program evaluation. In *The administration of mental health services.* S. Feldman, ed. Springfield, Ill.: Charles C. Thomas, 1973.

Borich, Gary D. A systems approach to the evaluation of training. In *Procedures for instructional systems development.* H. F. O'Neil, ed. New York: Academic Press, 1979.

Borus, Michael E., ed. *Evaluating the impact of manpower programs*. Lexington, Mass.: D. C. Heath & Co., 1972.

Borus, Michael E. *Measuring the impact of employment-related social programs*. Kalamazoo, Mich.: W. E. Upjohn Institute for Employment Research, 1979.

Brack, Robert. Innovative projects evaluation. *Journal of Extension*, 1975, *13*, 39–47.

Broskowski, A. Management information systems for planning and evaluation. In *Program evaluation in the health fields* 2nd ed. H. C. Schulberg & F. Baker, eds. New York: Behavioral Publications, 1979.

Bryk, A. S., et al. *The evaluation primer*. Planning report of the Brookline Early Education Project, Brookline, Mass., 1975.

Campbell, Donald T. From description to experimentation: Interpreting trends as quasi-experiments. In *Problems in measuring change*. C. W. Harris, ed. Madison, Wisc.: University of Wisconsin Press, 1963.

Campbell, Donald T. Quasi-experimental designs. In *Social experimentation as a method for planning and evaluating social programs*. H. W. Riecken et al., eds. New York: Academic Press, 1974.

Campbell, Donald T. Reforms as experiments. In *Handbook of evaluation research*, Vol. 1, Elmer L. Streuning & Marcia Guttentag, eds. Beverly Hills, Calif.: Sage Publications, 1975.

Campbell, Donald T. Focal local indicators for social program evaluation. *Social Indicators Research*, 1976, *3*, 237–256. Also in *Evaluation Studies Review Annual*, Vol. 2. Marcia Guttentag, ed. Beverly Hills, Calif.: Sage Publications, 1977.

Campbell, Donald T., & Boruch, Robert F. Making the case for random assignments. In *Evaluation and experiment*. C. A. Bennett and A. Lumsdaine, eds. New York: Academic Press, 1975.

Campbell, Donalt T., and Erlebacher, Albert. How regression artifacts in quasi-experimental evaluations can mistakenly make compensatory education look harmful. In *Handbook of evaluation research*. Vol. 1, Elmer Streuning & Marcia Guttentag, eds. Beverly Hills, Calif.: Sage Publications, 1975. Also in *The disadvantaged child*, Vol. 3: *Compensatory Education: A National Debate*. J. Hellmuth, ed. New York: Brunner/Mazel, 1970.

Campbell, Donald T., & Stanley, Julian C. *Experimental and quasi-experimental designs for research*. Chicago: Rand-McNally, 1966. Also in *Handbook of research on teaching*. N. L. Gage, ed. New York: Rand-McNally, 1963.

Cannel, Charles F., & Kahn, Robert L. Interviewing. In *The handbook of social psychology*, Vol. 2. Reading, Mass.: Addison-Wesley, 1968.

Caro, Francis G., ed. *Readings in evaluation research*, 2nd ed. New York: Russell Sage, 1977.

Carter, Reginald K. Clients' resistance to negative findings and the latent conservative function of evaluation studies. *American Sociologist*, 1971, *6*, 118–124.

Chelimsky, Eleanor. Differing Perspectives of Evaluation. In *New Directions for Program Evaluation*, Summer 1978, *2*, 1–18.

Cherney, Paul R., ed. *Making evaluation research useful*. Columbia, Md.: American City Corp., 1971.

Chommie, Peter W., & Hudson, Joe. Evaluation of outcome and process. *Social Work*, 1974, *19*, 682–687.

Cohen, David K. Politics and research: Evaluation of social action programs in education. *Review of Educational Research*, 1970, *40*, 213–238.

Cook, T. D., and Campbell, Donald T. The design and conduct of quasi-experiments and true experiments in field settings. In *Handbook of industrial and organizational research*. M. D. Dunnette, ed. Chicago: Rand-McNally, 1976.

Cooley, W. W., & Lohnes, P. R. *Evaluation research in education*. New York: Irvington, 1976.

Datta, Lois-Ellin. Does it work when it has been tried? and half full or half empty? *Journal of Career Education*, 1976, *2*, 38–55. Also in *Evaluation studies review annual*, Vol. 2. Marcia Guttentag, ed. Beverly Hills, Calif.: Sage Publications, 1977.

Datta, Lois-Ellin. Front-end analysis: Pegasus or shank's mare. *New Directions for Program Evaluation*, Spring 1978, *1*, 13–30.

Davis, Howard R., &Salasin, Susan E. The utilization of evaluation. In *Handbook of evaluation research*, Vol. 1. E. L. Streuning and Marcia Guttentag, eds. Beverly Hills, Calif.: Sage Publications, 1975.

Deutsch, S. J., & Alt, F. B. The effect of Massachusetts' gun control law on gun-related crimes in the City of Boston. *Evaluation Quarterly*, 1977, *1*, 543–568.

Deutscher, Irwin. Toward avoiding the goal trap in evaluation research. In *Readings in evaluation research*, 2nd ed. Francis G. Caro, ed. New York: Russell Sage, 1977.

Dipple, Gene, & House, William C. *Information systems: Data processing and evaluation*. Glenview, Ill.: Scott, Foresman & Co., 1969.

Dolbeare, Kenneth M., ed. *Public policy evaluation*. Beverly Hills, Calif.: Sage Publications, 1975.

Douglas, J. *Investigative social research*. Beverly Hills, Calif.: Sage Publications, 1976.

Ebel, R. L. *Measuring educational achievement*. Englewood Cliffs, N.J.: Prentice-Hall, 1965.

Fairweather, George. *Methods for experimental social innovation*. New York: Wiley, 1967.

Fairweather, George W., & Tornatzky, L. G. *Experimental methods for social policy research*. New York: Pergamon Press, 1977.

Ferman, Louis, A. Some perspectives on evaluating social welfare programs. *The Annals of the American Academy of Political and Social Science,* 1969, *385,* 143–156.

Fitz-Gibbon, Carol, and Morris, Lynn, *How to calculate statistics.* Vol. 7 in Program Evaluation Kit (8 volumes). Lynne L. Morris, ed. Beverly Hills, Calif.: Sage Publications, 1978.

Fitz-Gibbon, Carol, & Morris, Lynn. *How to design a program evaluation.* Vol. 3 in Program Evaluation Kit (8 volumes). Lynn L. Morris, ed. Beverly Hills, Calif.: Sage Publications, 1978.

Fry, Lincoln J. Participant observation and program evaluation. *Journal of Health and Social Behavior,* 1973, *14,* 274–278.

Furst, E. J. *Constructing evaluation instruments.* New York: David McKay, 1964.

Glaser, Daniel. *Routinizing evaluation: Getting feedback on effectiveness of crime and delinquency programs.* Washington, D.C.: U.S. Government Printing Office, 1973.

Glaser, Edward M., & Ross, Harvey L. *Increasing the utilization of applied research results.* Los Angeles, Calif.: Human Interaction Research Institute, 1971.

Green, J. L., and Stone, J. C. *Curriculum evaluation: Theory and practice.* New York: Springer, 1977.

Gurel, Lee. The human side of evaluating human services programs. In *Handbook of evaluation research,* Vol. 2. Marcia Guttentag & Elmer L. Struening, eds. Beverly Hills, Calif.: Sage Publications, 1975.

Guttentag, Marcia. Evaluations of social intervention programs. *Annals of the New York Academy of Sciences,* 1973, *218,* 3–13.

Guttentag, Marcia. Subjectivity and its uses in evaluation. *Evaluation,* 1973, *1,* 60–65.

Harless, J. H. An analysis of front-end analysis. *Improving Human Performance: A Research Quarterly,* 1973, *2,* 229–244.

Hatry, Harry P., et al. *Practical program evaluation for state and local government officials.* Washington, D.C.: The Urban Institute, 1973.

Hauser, P. M. *Social statistics in use.* New York: Russell Sage, 1975.

Heilman, John G. *Evaluation: A practical guide for evaluators of social action projects.* Auburn, Ala.: Auburn University Office of Public Service and Research, 1977.

Heineman, S., & Yudin, L. The consumer as evaluator: Perceptions and satisfaction level of former clients. *Journal of Community Psychology,* 1974, *2,* 21–23.

Henerson, Marlene, et al. *How to measure attitudes.* Vol. 5 in Program Evaluation Kit (8 volumes). Lynn L. Morris, ed. Beverly Hills, Calif.: Sage Publications, 1978.

Hetherington, Robert W., et al. The nature of program evaluation in mental health. *Evaluation*, 1974, *2*.

Hodges, Walter L., & Sheehan, Robert. Evaluation: Strategies for generating knowledge. *New directions for program evaluation*, Summer 1978, *2*, 81–93.

Hull, W. L., & Wells, R. L. *Innovations evaluation guide*. Columbus, Ohio: Center for Vocational and Technical Education, 1977.

Jemelka, Ron P., & Borich, Gary D. Traditional and emerging definitions of educational evaluation. *Evaluation Quarterly*, 1979, *3*, 263–276.

Johnson, John M. *Doing field research*. New York: The Free Press, 1975.

Kelling, G. L., et al. *The preventive patrol experiment*. Washington, D.C.: Police Foundation, 1974.

Kirby, Michael P. *The role of the administrator in evaluation*. Washington, D.C.: Pretrial Services Resource Center, 1979.

Kiresuk, Thomas J., & Sherman, R. E. Goal attainment scaling: A general method for evaluating community mental health programs. *Community Mental Health Journal*, 1968, *4*, 443–453.

Kiresuk, Thomas J., et al. Translating theory into practice: Change research at the Program Evaluation Research Center. *Evaluation and Change*, 1977, *4*, 89–95.

Klein, Malcolm W., & Teilmann, Katherine S., eds. *Handbook of criminal justice evaluation*. Beverly Hills, Calif.: Sage Publications, 1980.

Kogan, Leonard S., & Shyne, Ann W. Tender-minded and tough-minded approaches in evaluative research. *Welfare in Review*, 1966, *14*, 12–17.

Kutchinsky, B. The effect of easy availability of pornography on the incidence of sex crimes: The Danish experience. *Journal of Social Issues*, 1973, *29*, 163–181.

Landsberg, Gerald, et al. eds. *Evaluation in practice: A sourcebook of evaluation studies from mental health care systems in the U.S.* Washington, D.C.: U.S. Government Printing Office, 1979.

Levin, H. Cost-effective analysis in evaluation research. In *Handbook of Evaluation Research*, Vol. 2. M. Guttentag & E. L. Streuning, eds. Beverly Hills, Calif.: Sage Publications, 1975.

Levine, Abraham S. Cost-benefit analysis and social welfare program evaluation. *Social Service Review*, June 1968.

Levine, R. A., & Williams, A. P., Jr. *Making evaluation effective: A guide*. Santa Monica, Calif.: The Rand Corporation, 1971.

Levinson, Perry. Evaluation of social welfare programs: Two research models. *Welfare in Review*, December 1966.

Levitan, Sar A., & Wurzburg, Gregory. *Evaluating federal social programs: An uncertain art*. Kalamazoo, Mich.: W. E. Upjohn Institute for Employment Research, 1979.

Lichfield, Nathaniel, et al. *Evaluation in the planning process*. Elmsford, N.Y.: Pergamon Press, 1975.

Lewis, Joseph H. *Evaluation of experiments in policing: How do you begin?* Washington, D.C.: Police Foundation, 1972.

Lindley, D. *Making decisions*. New York: Wiley, 1971.

Logsdon, David. A practical look at evaluation. *Journal of Extension*, 1975, *13*, 31–38.

Longest, James. Designing evaluative research. *Journal of Extension*, 1975, *13*, 48–55.

Longwood, Robert, & Simmel, Arnold. Organizational resistance to innovation suggested by research. In *Evaluating action programs: Readings in social action and education*. Carol H. Weiss, ed. Boston: Allyn & Bacon, 1972.

Lorei, T. W., & Schroeder, N. H. Integrating program evaluation and medical audit. *Hospital and Community Psychiatry*, 1975, *26*, 733–735.

Lucas, Henry C. *Why information systems fail*. New York: Columbia University Press, 1975.

Mangum, Garth L. Evaluating manpower programs. *Monthly Labor Review*. February 1968.

Mangum, Garth, & Walsh, John. *Employment and training programs for youth: What works best for whom?* Washington, D.C.: U.S. Government Printing Office, 1978.

Mann, John. Technical and social difficulties in the conduct of evaluative research. In *Readings in Evaluation Research*. Francis Caro, ed. New York: Russell Sage, 1971.

Mass, A. Benefit-cost analysis: Its relevance to public investment decisions. *Quarterly Journal of Economics*, May 1966.

Miller, S. M. The study of man: Evaluating action programs. *Transaction*, March–April 1965.

Mitre Corp., The. *Evaluation in criminal justice programs: Guidelines and examples*. Washington, D.C.: U.S. Government Printing Office, 1973.

Morris, Albert. A correctional adminstrators' guide to the evaluation of correctional programs. *Correctional Research*, 1971, Bulletin No. 21, 1–35.

Morris, Lynn L., ed. *Program evaluation kit* (8 volumes). Beverly Hills, Calif.: Sage Publications, 1978.

Morris, Lynn, & Fitz-Gibbon, Carol. *Evaluator's handbook*. Vol. 1 in Program Evaluation Kit (8 volumes). Lynn L. Morris, ed. Beverly Hills, Calif.: Sage Publications, 1978.

Morris, Lynn, & Fitz-Gibbon, Carol. *How to deal with goals and objectives*. Vol. 2 in Program Evaluation Kit (8 volumes). Lynn L. Morris, ed. Beverly Hills, Calif.: Sage Publications, 1978.

Morris, Lynn, & Fitz-Gibbon, Carol. *How to measure program implementation*. Vol. 4 in Program Evaluation Kit (8 volumes). Lynn L. Morris, ed. Beverly Hills, Calif.: Sage Publications, 1978.

Morris, Lynn, & Fitz-Gibbon, Carol. *How to measure achievement*. Vol. 6 in Program Evaluation Kit (8 volumes). Lynn L. Morris, ed. Beverly Hills, Calif.: Sage Publications, 1978.

Morris, Lynn, & Fitz-Gibbon, Carol. *How to present an evaluation report*. Vol. 8 in Program Evaluation Kit (8 volumes). Lynn L. Morris, ed. Beverly Hills, Calif.: Sage Publications, 1978.

Moursund, Janet P. *Evaluation: An introduction to research design*. Monterey, Calif.: Brooks/Cole, 1973.

Moynihan, Daniel P. The crisis of confidence. In *The Use of Social Research in Federal Domestic Programs*. Washington, D.C.: U.S. Government Printing Office, April 1967.

Mushkin, Selma J. Evaluations: Use with caution. *Evaluation*, 1973, *1*.

National Institute of Mental Health. *Planning for creative change in mental health services: Use of program evaluation*. Washington, D.C.: U.S. Government Printing Office, 1971.

Neigher, W., et al., eds. *Emerging developments in mental health program evaluation*. New York: Argold Press, 1977.

Orlans, Harold. *Contracting for knowledge*. San Francisco: Jossey-Bass Publishers, 1973.

Page, S., & Yates, E. Fear of evaluation and reluctance to participate in research. *Professional Psychology*, November 1974.

Polgar, Steven, & Kaffe, F. S. Evaluation and record keeping for U.S. family planning services. *Public Health Reports*, August 1968.

Prest, A. R., & Turvey, Ralph. Cost-benefit analysis: A survey. In *Surveys of economic theory*, Vol. 3 New York: St. Martin's Press, 1967.

Richardson, S. A., et al. *Interviewing: Its forms and functions*. New York: Basic Books, 1965.

Riecken, H. W., & Boruch, Robert F. *Social experimentation: A method for planning and evaluating social intervention*. New York: Academic Press, 1974.

Rivlin, Alice. *Systematic thinking for social action*. Washington, D.C.: The Brookings Institution, 1971.

Rivlin, Alice, et al. *Protecting individual privacy in evaluation research*. Washington, D.C.: National Research Council, 1975.

Roos, Leslie L. Jr., et al. Using administrative data banks for research and evaluation: A case study. *Evaluation Quarterly*, 1979, *3*, 236–255.

Rosenblatt, Aaron. The practitioner's use and evaluation of research. *Social Work*, 1968, *13*, 53–59.

Ross, H. L., & Campbell, D. T. The Connecticut speed crackdown: A study of the effects of legal change. In *Perspectives on the social order*. H. L. Ross, ed. New York: McGraw-Hill, 1968.

Ross, H. L., et al. Determining the social effects of a legal reform: The British

Breathalyzer Crackdown of 1967. *American Behavioral Scientist*, 1979, *13*, 493–509.

Rossi, Peter H., & Williams, W., eds. *Evaluating social programs*. New York: Seminar, 1972.

Rossi, Peter H., et al. *Evaluation: A systematic approach*. Beverly Hills, Calif.: Sage Publications, 1979.

Rossi, Peter H., et al., eds. *Handbook of survey research*. New York: Academic Press, 1979.

Roth, Jane. Needs and the needs assessment process. *Evaluation News*, 1978, *5*, 15.

Rutman, Leonard, ed. *Evaluation research methods: A basic guide*. Beverly Hills, Calif.: Sage Publications, 1977.

Sackman, H. *Planning, management and evaluation of community action programs*. Santa Monica, Calif.: The Rand Corp., 1973.

Schatzman, L., & Strauss, A. L. *Field research: Strategies for a natural sociology*. Englewood Cliffs, N.J.: Prentice-Hall, 1973.

Schick, Allen. Evaluating evaluation: A Congressional perspective. In *Legislative oversight and program evaluation*. Washington, D.C.: U.S. Government Printing Office, May 1976.

Schulberg, H. C., et al., eds. *Program evaluation in the health fields*. New York: Behavioral Publications, 1969.

Scriven, Michael. The methodology of evaluation. In *Curriculum evaluation: American educational research association monograph series on evaluation*, No. 1. R. E. Stake, ed. Chicago: Rand-McNally, 1976. Also in *Evaluating action programs: Readings in social action and education*. C. H. Weiss, ed. Boston: Allyn & Bacon, 1972.

Scriven, Michael. Goal-free evaluation. In *School evaluation*. Ernest R. House, ed. Berkeley, Calif.: McCutchan, 1973.

Scriven, Michael. Evaluation bias and its control. In *Evaluation studies review annual*, Vol. 2. Gene V. Glass, ed. Beverly Hills, Calif.: Sage Publications, 1976.

Scriven, Michael, & Roth, Jane. Needs assessment. *Evaluation News*, 1976, *2*, 25–28.

Scriven, Michael, & Roth, Jane. Needs assessment: Concept and practice. *New Directions for Program Evaluation*, 1978, *1*, 1–11.

Shortell, S. M., & Richardson, W. C. *Health program evaluation*. St. Louis: Mosby, 1978.

Slocum, W. L. Sociological research for action agencies: Some guides and hazards. *Rural Sociology*, 1956, *21*, 196–199.

Smith, Wiley C. *An introductin to evaluation research for agency administrators*. Cincinnati, Ohio: International Halfway House Association.

Stake, R. E. Objectives, priorities, and other judgment data. *Review of Educational Research,* 1970, *40,* 181–212.

Stone, James C. E-VALUE-ation. *New Directions for Program Evaluation,* Spring 1978, *1,* 73–82.

Stufflebeam, D. L., et al. *Educational evaluation and decision-making.* Itasca, Ill.: Peacock, 1971.

Suchman, Edward A. *Evaluative research: Principles and practice in public service and social action programs.* New York: Russell Sage Foundation, 1967.

Suchman, Edward A. Action for what: A critique of evaluative research. In *Evaluating action programs: Readings in social action and education.* C. H. Weiss, ed. Boston: Allyn & Bacon, 1972.

Sze, William C., & Hopps, June G. eds. *Evaluation and accountability in human service programs.* Cambridge, Mass.: Schenkman Publishing Co., 1974.

Walker, R. A. The ninth panacea: Program evaluation. *Evaluation,* 1972, *1,* 45–53.

Webb, E. J., Campbell, D. T., Schwartz, R. E., & Sechrest, L. B. *Unobtrusive measures: Nonreactive research in the social sciences.* Chicago: Rand-McNally, 1966.

Weick, Karl E. Systematic observational methods. In *The handbook of social psychology,* Vol. 2. G. Lindzey and E. Aronson, eds. Reading, Mass.: Addison-Wesley, 1968.

Weinberg, Eve. *Community surveys with local talent.* Chicago: National Opinion Research Center, 1971.

Weiss, Carol H. Planning an action project evaluation. In *Learning in Action.* June L. Shmelzer, ed. Washington, D.C.: U.S. Government Printing Office, 1966.

Weiss, Carol H. *Evaluation research: Methods of assessing program effectiveness.* Englewood Cliffs, N.J.: Prentice Hall, 1972.

Weiss, Carol H. *Evaluating action programs: Readings in social action and education.* Boston: Allyn & Bacon, 1972.

Weiss, Carol H. Where politics and evaluation research meet. *Evaluation,* 1973, *1.*

Weiss, Carol H. Interviewing in evaluation research. In *Handbook of Evaluation Research,* Vol. 1, Elmer L. Streuning & Marcia Guttentag, eds. Beverly Hills, Calif.: Sage Publications, 1975.

Weiss, Robert S., & Rein, Martin. Evaluation of broad-aim programs: Experimental design, its difficulties, and an alternative. *Administrative Science Quarterly,* 1970, *15,* 97–109.

Westin, A. F., & Baker, M. A. *Data books in a free society.* New York; Quadrangle, 1972.

Wholey, Joseph S. What can we actually get from program evaluation? *Policy Sciences,* 1972, *3,* 361–369.

Wholey, J. S. Evaluability assessment. In *Evaluation research methods: A basic guide*. L. Rutman, ed. Beverly Hills, Calif.: Sage Publications, 1977.

Wholey, Joseph S., et al. *Federal evaluation policy: Analyzing the effects of public programs*. Washington, D.C.: The Urban Institute, 1973.

Wildavksy, Aaron. The self-evaluating organization. *Public Administration Review*, 1972, September/October.

Wilkinson, G. L. Needed; Information for cost analysis. *Educational Technology*, 1972, *12*, 33–38.

Williams, Walter. Developing an agency evaluation strategy for social action programs. *The Journal of Human Resources*, 1969, *4*.

Williams, Walter, & Evans, John W. The politics of evaluation: The case of Head Start. *Annals of the American Academy of Political and Social Science*, 1969, *385*, 118–132.

Wilner, Daniel M., et al. Databank of program evaluations. *Evaluation*, 1973, *1*.

Windle, C., & Neigher, W. Ethical problems in program evaluation: Advice for trapped evaluators. *Evaluation and Program Planning*, 1978, *1*, 97–107.

Worthen, B. R., & Sanders, J. R. *Educational evaluation: Theory and practice*. Worthington, Ohio: Charles A. Jones, 1973.

Wortman, Paul M. Evaluation research: A pscyhological perspective. *American Psychologist*, May 1975, 562–575.

INDEX

INDEX

Accountability, evaluation research and, 11–12
Action/research consortium, 29
Advocacy position, 9
Attitudinal questions, costs of collecting, 64
Auditing, of evaluation data and fieldwork, 77

Baseline data, program data compared with, 21–23
Before-and-after studies, 67–68
Bias
  of evaluators, 13–14
  in interpretation of statistics, 82
Bibliography, 89–99
Bids, for contract with evaluator, 43

Case studies, 69

Categorical variable, 58
Chi-square test, 79
Clerical personnel, 51
Client characteristics, as variables, 59
Common sense, evaluation research planning and, 32–33
Comparison data, control groups and, 59–60, 68
Computer analysis, 80–81
Computer simulations, 71
Computerized data
  costs of, 50
  of private or government agencies, 27–28
Computer programs
  for evaluation research, 30
  ready-made packages, 80
  See also Computers
Computers, 12–13

(Computers *Con't.*)
  shared, 52
  See also Computer analysis;
      Computer simulations; Com-
      puterized data; Computer
      programs
Conclusiveness of study, research
    scope and, 33–34
Confidentiality. *See* Privacy
Contract with evaluator, 43–44
Control groups, 59–60
  cooperation of, 61
  denial of services to, 61
  experimental design and, 60–61,
      68–69
Cost-benefit analysis, 70
Cost effectiveness, 70
  evaluation and, 11–12
  in-house research and, 45
Costs
  of data collection, 64
  of program, analysis of, 69–70
  of interviewers, 77
  and ready-made computer prog-
      rams, 80
  See also Cost-benefit analysis;
      Cost effectiveness; Evalua-
      tion research costs
Credibility, in-house research and,
    45

Data
  confidentiality of, 76
  errors in, 18–19
  falsification of, 45, 77
  interpretation of, *see* Data
      analysis
  from prior studies, 26
  of private or government agen-
      cies, 27–28
  programs compared to "baseline,"
      21–22

  quality of, 18–20
  report format of, 23–24
  sources of, 19–20, 34, 36–37, 65
  summaries of, 37
  See also Data collection; Data
      processing
Data analysis, 18, 78–82
  data interpretation and, 81–82
Data collection
  for comparison group studies, 68
  experts and, 39
  in field, 73
  and nature of program questions,
      62–64
  See also Data collectors
Data collectors
  costs of, 48–49
  stage of introduction of, 50
Data processing, cost of, 52–53
Data-processing experts, 39
Data size, computer analysis and,
    80, 81
Deadlines, 40
  in contract, 43–44
Dependent variables, 58
Distribution of final report, 85–86
Documentation
  of evaluation research, 44
  of field work, 73–74
Drop outs, 61

Editing, of final report, 85
Evaluation research
  accountability and, 11–12
  analysis of program costs and,
      69–70
  avoidance of repetition of, 25–31
  before-and-after studies, 67–68
  bibliography on, 89–99
  budgeting for, 39, *see also* Eva-
      luation research costs
  case studies, 69

compared with statistics, 15–24
comparison-group studies, 68
computer analysis and, 80–81
and computerized data bases of
    private or government orga-
    nizations, 27–28
and conflicts between research
    and program operation, 75–76
contract for, 43–44
and data analysis, 78–82
and data interpretation, 81–82
and deadlines, 77
documentation of, 73–74
experiments, 60–61, 68–69
and experts, *see* Experts
and field data collection, 73
final report, *see* Final report
funding of, *see* Funding
and hidden agendas, 12–14
and information system data, 20–
    24, 36–37
in house, 44–47
innovative, 70–71
as joint venture with com-
    plementary groups, 28–29
legal problems of, 76
maintenance of control of, 73–74
personnel for, 30–31
in phases, 37
and pilot testing, 72–73
planning for, *see* Evaluation re-
    search planning
and preconceptions, 13
prior, 25–27
purpose of, 9–14
and reports of similar agencies,
    27–28
representative methods for, 36–37
role of, 10
selection of methods for, 35–36
and statistical significance, 79–80
and time-series analysis, 22–23

timing problems and, 34–35
unneeded, 11
and use of publications, reports
    and computer programs, 29–
    30
See also Evaluation research
    costs; Evaluation research
    reports
Evaluation research administrator,
    48
Evaluation research costs
data processing, 52–53
drop outs and, 61
experiments, 60
federal funding of, 53–55
major, 48–50
reduction of, 50–52
See also Costs
Evaluation research planning, 62–66
changes in, 74–75
and concept papers from prospec-
    tive consultants, 41–42
expert assistance with, 38–39
and focus of study, 32–33
and prediction of findings, 65–66
program questions and, 62–64
revision of, 72–73
and scope of study, 33–34
and usefulness of findings, 64–65
Evaluation research reports
readability of, 56–57
research terms used in, 57–60
usefulness of, 64–65
Evaluators
bias of, 13–14
contract with, 43–44
See also Experts
Executive summary, 84–85
in contract, 44
Experiments, 60–61, 68–69
Experts
in computer analysis, 80

(Experts *Con't.*)
   contracts with, 43–44
   costs of, 48–50
   in data collection, 39
   and language of reports, 56–57
   loan of, 51
   part-timers, 50–51
   and planning stage, 38–39
   reduction of costs of, 50–52
   relationship with organization,
      42–43
   selection of, 40–42
   in statistics and data processing,
      39
   writers, 40

Federal Register, 54
Fieldwork, 73
   auditing of, 77
   compared with laboratory re-
      search, 31
Final report
   in contract, 44
   distribution of, 85–86
   editing of, 85
   executive summary of, 44, 84–85
   personal briefings and presenta-
      tions of, 86
   preparation of, 84–85
   previews of, 83–84
Findings. *See* Final report
Focus of research, 32–33
"Formative" evaluation research. *See*
   Operations-type evaluation research
Funding, 12
   federal, 53–55
   private, 54–55
   proposal writing for, 39
   and timing of research, 34

Glossary of terms, 57

Grants. *See* Funding

Hidden agendas, evaluation and, 12–
   14
How to Lie With Statistics (Huff),
   82
Huff, Darrel, 82

Information-collection, interviews of
   staff and clients for, 36
   See also Data collection; Inter-
      viewers; Interviews
Information systems
   and answers to questions, 15–18
   design of, evaluation research
      and, 21
   and interpretation of data, 18
   modification or reprogramming
      of, 23
   and privacy problems, 20
   and quality of data, 18–20
   usefulness for evaluation research,
      20–24, 36–37
Informed consent, 76
Interim reports, 74
Interviewers
   costs of, 49
   payment by hour vs. per inter-
      view, 77
   See also Interviews
Interviews
   costs of, 61
   in dangerous settings, 76
   and quality of data, 19–20

Jargon, in research reports, 56–57
Joint evaluation research, 28–29, 50,
   52

Keypunching
   costs, 53
   errors, 19

Laboratory research, compared with field research, 31
Lawyer, and contract for evaluation research, 43
Legal problems, 76
Liability, for safety of interviewers, 76

Management consultants
  for evaluation research, 40–41
  and personnel costs, 49
  previous research by, 26
Media, research reports to, 85–86

Natural experiments, 61
Nominal variable, 58

Observation studies, 32–33
Operations-type evaluation research
  questions initiating, 10
  and scope of study, 33
Optical scanning, 53

Part-time personnel, 50–51
Personal briefings and presentations, 86
Personnel
  for evaluation research, 30–31, 48–49
  link between information-system data and program questions and, 17–18
  program questions and, 11
  relationship with experts, 42–43
  See also Experts; Staff
Pilot tests, 72–73
Policy decisions, evaluation research results and, 86
Preconceptions, 13
Privacy issues, 76
  information-system data and, 20

Professionals. See Experts; Staff
Program changes, 75
Program evaluation. See Evaluation research
Program formulation, questions on, 10
Program impact
  design and, 63–64
  information systems data and, 16
  in-house research on, 45
  questions on, 9–10
  and scope of study, 33
Program operations
  conflict with research needs, 75–76
  information system data and, 16
Programs
  questions about, see Questions about programs
  staff and client perception of, 36
  See also Program changes; Program formulation; Program impact; Program operations
PROMIS system, 22–23
Prosecutor's Management Information System. See PROMIS system
Public agencies, program evaluation in. See Evaluation research

Questions about programs
  answers to, data analysis and, 78
  changes in, 74–75
  evaluation research to answer, 9–11, 32–34
  formulation of, 9–11
  information systems and, 15–18, 21
  new, research scope and, 34
  research design and, 62–64
  selection of research method and, 35–36
  value-related, 10

"Quick and dirty" studies, 33–34

Random assignment, 60
Random sample, 57
Recidivism, measurement of, 59
Reliability of data, 19
Representative sample, 57
Reproducibility of data, 19
Research managers and analysts,
    cost of, 49

Samples
    defined, 57–58
    size of, 57–58
Scope of research, 33–34
Services, denial to control group, 61
Shared research. *See* Joint evalua-
    tion research
Social scientists
    laboratory and field research of,
        31
    selection of, 41
"Software houses," 53
SPSS, 50
Staff
    involvement in evaluation re-
        search, 46
    See also In-house evaluation re-
        search
Statistical Package for the Social
    Sciences. *See* SPSS
Statistical significance, 59, 79–80

Statistical tests, 78–80
    See also Data analysis
Statistics, compared with evaluation
    research, 15–24
Students, evaluation research by, 51
Surveys, 39

Telephone interviews, 63
Time-series analysis, 22–23
    and before-and-after studies, 67–
        68
Timing problems, 34–35
"t-test," 78–79
Travel expenses of interviewers, 49
Troubleshooting
    and conflicts between research
        and program operations, 75–
        76
    and legal problems, 76

Unintended side effects of program,
    11, 75
University research groups, 40
    indirect costs of, 49–50

Validity of data, 19–20
Variables, 58–59
    statistical significance of, 59

Writer of evaluation report, 40
    See also Final report